Dynamic Fingertip Devotions

DYNAMIC
FINGERTIP DEVOTIONS

Amy Bolding

BAKER BOOK HOUSE
Grand Rapids, Michigan 49506

This book is dedicated
to two very dear friends,
MR. AND MRS. J. D. MC PHAUL,
who plant seeds of kindness and love
wherever they go.

Paperback edition issued April 1977

Library of Congress Catalog Card Number 73-78081

ISBN: 0-8010-0708-9

First printing, April 1977
Second printing, June 1979
Third printing, September 1980
Fourth printing, January 1983
Fifth printing, August 1984

Contents

1

How Beautiful Are the Clouds!

Dost thou know the balancings of the clouds, the wondrous works of him which is perfect in knowledge? —Job 37:16

Are there no clouds in your sky? How boring life would be if there were no clouds, no problems to meet!

While visiting for the church one day, I came to the home of a woman past ninety years of age. She was happy and busy. She had made an afghan for each of her granddaughters and was starting to make one for each of her great-grandchildren.

"You certainly do like bright, beautiful colors!" I said as I admired the vivid yellow and blue yarn.

"I just refuse to work on drab colors. I don't want any darkness about the things I make," was her reply.

On another occasion, at an art exhibit I admired a still life. I felt the artist had been especially skillful from the standpoint of the shadow. The vase in her painting looked beautiful, but just behind it she had painted a perfect shadow.

I looked in admiration from the painting to the artist. "For me, the shadow makes the picture come alive," I exclaimed.

"Oh, yes," she replied, "shadows bring life and movement to any picture. I try to balance mine—not too much, yet enough for contrast."

She went on talking about art and how she handled her colors. I started thinking of life, and the lives I touched each day. Not many people I know live a cloudless existence.

Not many artists try to paint a picture without some type of cloud or shadow. In a similar manner, the Artist of all of life balances the clouds in the lives of His children. He wants us to be beautiful and effective examples to a lost world.

I have taught adult women in Sunday school for many years. It amazes me when we come to the end of a year to look back and see the clouds and sunshine that have come and gone over the women in my class.

I often stand amazed at the grace and poise some women possess in time of sorrow or disaster. At other times I am disappointed and hurt when I see some person I thought to be a strong Christian, crumble and go to pieces in the face of problems.

Looking back over life from many years of clouds and sunshine, I am grateful to God for the clouds. They often seem so dark at the moment, but the sunshine looks twice as bright when the clouds have passed over.

Once on a plane trip from Texas to California, we flew above the clouds. It seemed as if we were just floating along on faintly tinted snow banks. I felt as if God was there by my side, telling me to behold the majesty of His creation.

There are times when life's clouds make us see a richer, better way to serve God and our fellow man.

A middle-aged couple were having trouble. The wife was considering a divorce. They had enough money to live in a comfortable fashion and lots of leisure to enjoy travel and hobbies; yet they were bored with each other.

One day a call came for the wife to rush to the hospital. Her husband had been seriously hurt in an accident.

For months she visited her husband daily in the hospital. His long stay there had greatly depleted their finances. As she waited by his bedside day after day, she could not help but meet other people in the hospital. The selfish, bored woman began to see life in a different way.

"I didn't need a divorce," she told her pastor, "I needed a purpose in life. If my husband lives, I will try to make his life pleasant and happy."

How sad it is that we must often have an ominous cloud hang over our lives in order to make us see our blessings.

Some of us want our lives to be like the lady who told about her fishing trip. "I drove to the lake in an air-conditioned car. My husband put a folding chair on the bank, and over it he placed a huge umbrella. Then he baited my hook and stood the pole in a socket by the chair."

"Did you have lots of fun?"

"No, I just leaned back and went to sleep."

The people who refuse to participate in any of the problems of life—who just lean back in ease and go to sleep—are missing one of life's greatest satisfactions: facing a challenge triumphantly.

While the lady slept, her husband went up the bank and had a grand time catching fish. He met some other fishermen and enjoyed the rest of the afternoon swapping fish stories with them.

Life was not meant to be without clouds—clouds to give beauty and depth of understanding, clouds to make us see and appreciate the good times we enjoy.

When the children of Israel were hungry in the desert, they complained against God, "though he had commanded the clouds from above, and opened the doors of heaven" (Ps. 78:23). God had given the people water from a rock, He had gone in a cloud over them to give them shade from the hot desert sun, yet they complained and doubted His mercies.

We condemn the Israelites for the ungrateful way they acted. Yet how often when a cloud comes to our life we complain against God.

Thank God for clouds to make us look up and depend on His abiding strength. We cannot solve our problems in our own might. "Ascribe ye strength unto God: his excellency is over Israel, and his strength is in the clouds" (Ps. 68:34).

Talking with an elderly woman after the funeral of her husband, I heard her say, "We walked hand in hand through many dark clouds, but to be alone without my husband is the darkest of all."

For any person to walk through a cloud of sorrow or tragedy without God is a very sad thing indeed.

MY BLESSED HEAVENLY FATHER

My blessed Heavenly Father,
Who daily walks with me,
Provides the Holy Spirit
My constant guide to be
While with his faithful presence
He keeps me company
Along my tortuous way.

My blessed Heavenly Father
Fills life up to the brim;
He helps me solve my problems
However dark and grim,
And makes each wondrous moment
A precious time with him,
To bid me near him stay.

His patience and his blessing
Amaze and gratify;
His saving love so thrilling
No word can amplify;
His gracious grace so filling,
Helps me to magnify
Each hour of every day.

My blessed Heavenly Father
Will love me to the end;
And then one of his angels
For me he'll surely send
To bring me home to heaven,
Where with the Lord I'll spend
One grand, eternal day!

—J. T. Bolding

2

Keep Walking On

I will walk before the Lord in the land of the living. —Psalm 116:9

O house of Jacob, come ye, and let us walk in the light of the Lord. —Isaiah 2:5

There is an old proverb that says, Though God may seem to frown in His providences, yet He always smiles in His promises.

Do you ever feel like quitting? Yet you keep walking on. What a poor world this would be if people quit every time they felt like it. The secret to a happy useful life is found in our Scripture: "Walk before the Lord."

Many famous men gained their place in history because they kept walking on, even after they had failed.

The famous ball player, Babe Ruth, struck out 1,330 times. Yet we never think of the times he struck out. We remember him for the 714 times he made home runs. What if he had said, "I struck out! I'll never play ball again!"

To live is to strike out sometimes, but to live well is to keep walking on in spite of a few failures.

Abraham Lincoln was a very poor young man. He was not an

attractive person physically, he failed when he ran for the legislature in Illinois, and he failed in a business venture.

He had several other failures, but he kept trying. He kept studying and striving for a goal. Finally he reached the presidency of our country, and he will always live in the hearts of Americans.

How can I keep walking on? you may ask when it seems you have more than your share of troubles and setbacks.

You might try like one little boy did. After the first snowstorm of the season, he went to shovel a path to his grandfather's door.

The grandfather looked out and called, "Your shovel is too small; you are too small; give it up."

"Grandfather, this shovel is my size; and by keeping at the snow I'll get you a path shoveled." The little boy kept right on shoveling. In a few hours he had a clean path shoveled up to his grandfather's door. The old man was delighted. He rewarded the child with a crisp dollar bill.

Many people give up in life because they stop and look at their shovel. It looks too small. Perhaps they are not as well educated as others. Perhaps they do not have the same quality or quantity of clothes as others around them.

Other people look about and see that there are better things and ways in life than they possess; so they set their goals and keep striving to reach them.

The newspapers recently carried a story about a five-year-old boy saving the life of his baby sister. The boy had been out near the road watching his parents push the family car, trying to start it. When the car was pushed out of sight, the child looked back at their house. What he saw made him run toward the house, for flames were licking at the shingles. He sped to the front door to rescue his little sister. The flames were so intense he could not get in. But he didn't stop trying; instead, he ran to the kitchen door and was able to get to the baby and carry her to safety. How grateful the parents were that their son kept trying to save his sister!

It was not easy for a five-year-old to go into a burning house. His great love for the baby gave him the determination to succeed.

If we have determined to walk with the Lord and in His will, we will not stop when adversity comes our way. We will just keep walking on.

We should stop from time to time and see if we are going in the right direction. Walking is worse than useless if we are going the wrong way. A man in Wise County, Texas, has worked forty years collecting maps, data, old folks' tales, and other tips about a treasure buried in that county. He thinks he has at one time been very near the treasure, but he has not yet found it.

Perhaps we are sometimes seeking only imaginary treasures. The Savior told us to seek a treasure called the kingdom of heaven. If we keep walking in the direction of that treasure, we are assured of a great reward.

Not only should we be sure we are walking in the right direction, we should be sure we are seeking the right destination.

On Sunday morning when I go to my department in Sunday school, I see two vacant rooms, opening off the assembly room. These rooms would easily care for a class of twenty-five each. Why are they not filled? We live in a city where it is estimated one hundred thousand people stay home each Sunday.

The rooms are not filled because we as teachers and leaders have not kept walking on—walking on into the streets and byways to invite and enlist more people. My room is filled each Sunday; why should I worry about two vacant rooms? That attitude may account for many empty rooms in churches across the land.

There is a big world outside our own home, our own town, our own state, waiting to be conquered, waiting to help someone to walk in the light of the Lord.

When you get a spell of despondency and want to quit, think about the beautiful sun. It sinks out of sight every night; but when morning comes, there it is again.

The little boy shoveling snow had a shovel to help him keep going. The child who saved his sister had a heart filled with love to give him courage. If you are a child of God, you too have some things to help you along the way. You have prayer. You have hope. You have His understanding and love. You have the wonderful guidebook called the

Bible. You have the promise of peace and comfort. How can you fail to be steadfast when God is walking by your side?

Your life is a success or a failure, not by what you have in your hand at birth, but by the spirit in your heart.

DID YOU EVER?

Did you ever feel that living
Was a hopeless drudge and chore?
Did you ever feel that giving
Was a pointless kind of bore?

Did you ever think that duty
Was too much for you to do,
And the search for truth and beauty
Was too big a task for you?

Did you ever think that others
Have provided very much,
And that you might owe your brothers
To provide for them some such?

Did you ever mention
How much God has done for you,
And there could be some contention
That you owe him something, too?

Don't give up nor be a quitter;
Keep on plugging and you'll see,
You will lose the taste of bitter
And your life will sweeter be.

—J. T. Bolding

3
Your Crystal Ball

And they said, Go to, let us build us a city and a tower, whose top may reach unto heaven; and let us make us a name, lest we be scattered abroad upon the face of the whole earth. —Genesis 11:4

Often a young person becomes impatient and wishes he could look into the future. He wants a crystal ball to reveal all the great things he will accomplish in the years to come.

Crystal balls are not God's plans. Going out to accomplish things in our own power is not God's way. The people in the Scripture verses above wanted to accomplish several things. They wanted to build a city, a tower, a way to reach into heaven. In the building of the city they wanted to make a name for themselves. They wanted to remain together and never go out into the broad world.

A small poem describes the attitude of the people who sought to build the tower.

> *Beware of too sublime a sense* ,
> *Of your own worth and consequence.*
> *The man who deems himself so great,*
> *And his importance of such weight,*

That all around in all that's done
Must move and act for him alone;
Will learn in school of tribulation
The folly of his expectation.

—William Cowper

What do you want from that crystal ball? from life? In the spring a youth wants love. In winter an old man wants peace and comfort. At all times a hermit wants to be alone. A child wants always to play.

A real child of God wants to serve and follow Him. The children of the tower of Babel did not stop to ask God what they could do to serve Him. They thought of a great plan that would make them famous.

In some of our American cities we have governments managed by men who do not think of the good they can accomplish for the needy in the city. They think of some great and expensive project they can build that will make them popular with the rich.

How many Christians fail to think of the good they can do, of the lost they can win! Instead, they think of how elegant they look as they go in fine clothes to sit in the pew each Sunday. If they could peer into a crystal ball, many people who are sitting in a prominent place on Sunday might read the words, "Depart from me, I never knew you."

How can we know God's plan for our lives? We can seek it. Some of the kingdom's most useful people started out in a small way, with small things. They tried to do the small tasks they were given to do in a hearty way; so God gave them bigger tasks.

Proverbs 29:23 reads: "A man's pride shall bring him low: but honour shall uphold the humble in spirit."

In her book *The Mill on the Floss,* George Eliot has one character, a haughty girl, say this line: "Know that the lofe of self doth hurt thee more than anything in the world."

How many people fail to look at the crystal ball of the future and realize that they are spending too much time on the pleasures of this world. They fail to see the inevitable consequences of drink, lust, and worldly desires.

A beautiful young girl, looking in the mirror, was pleased with what she saw. Her eyes were clearest blue, her hair was golden brown. Not a blemish was on her lovely face. As she was contemplating what she saw, she remembered a temptation to smoke some marijuana. Thinking of the place she planned to meet her friends and experiment, she suddenly saw the image in front of her become distorted and clouded. Her younger sister had turned on the hot water in the bathtub and steam had covered the mirror.

"My mind might be like that mirror if I go with my friends." She picked up a towel and wiped the mirror. Her image was still distorted. "I will not go!" she declared.

On the late news that evening as the beautiful blue-eyed girl sat with her family in the living room she heard a startling thing: some young people had been caught in a vacant house smoking pot. One girl had been rushed to the hospital in serious condition. Some of the boys were in jail.

"Was that where you said you would not go?" the younger sister asked.

"Yes, it was. They will never be my friends again. I'm so glad I didn't go. The mirror warned me not to go."

"God warned you, dear," her mother said. "He only used the mirror to get the message across."

"When I told them no at school they made fun of me and said I was a chicken."

"You were the brave one," her father told her. "It is cowardice to go with the crowd every time."

There are a few ways we can look into the future. We can listen to those who have had experience and know what the road ahead looks like.

We are living in a day when the young think any person past thirty is not, in their language, "with it." Yet an older person can remember some of the pitfalls of life and can warn against some common mistakes.

The pastor is always a good person with whom to talk over plans. He has had experience with many people and knows the basic problems you will encounter in the future. He also knows the One who holds the future and can talk to Him about you.

Then there is the great and wonderful guidebook, the Bible. What better way to learn about the future than to read each day from the Book!

Just outside our back door there is a rose bush. Often when my husband goes off to work he clips a rose and takes it to his office. One day I watched him clip a very tight bud. The next day I happened to stop by his office; and there on the desk was a beautiful, full-blown rose.

"Don't tell me this is the bud you cut yesterday!" I said.

"Yes; and isn't it pretty?"

I think God's plans for your life and mine are like the rosebud. We cannot tear the petals open; they must open as we go along, as God sees we are ready for advancement or change.

Then last but greatest of all is the way of planning your future through prayer. Many people have found in prayer an answer to problems, to plans, to the solving of difficult situations. Always pray about any problem or plan. God will lead you in the right direction.

BURNING BUSHES

A flaming bush for everyone
Is set within plain view,
Where God reveals what he wants done
If we will follow through.

That burning bush in your own heart
The still small voice may be,
As conscience surely does its part
To speak for God, you see.

Again that flaming bush for you
May speak through circumstance
Or through some deep desire that grew,
As if by happenstance.

That burning bush could also be
A dear friend's godly voice,

And in the Bible we may see
God's word to help our choice.

Hark, there's a flaming bush, and so,
Take off your shoes, draw near,
And seek God's precious will to know
As his dear voice you hear.

—J. T. Bolding

4
Misplaced Hands

And Israel stretched out his right hand, and laid it upon Ephraim's head, who was the younger, and his left hand upon Manasseh's head, guiding his hands wittingly; for Manasseh was the firstborn. —Genesis 48:14

Manasseh and Ephraim were the sons of Joseph. Their grandfather Jacob, or Israel as he was called in later life, met them when he was carried to Egypt because of the great famine. When Jacob stretched out his right hand to the younger grandson, Ephraim, it meant the greater blessing was going to the younger.

Later in the history of the Hebrew people we find Ephraim's tribe having ascendancy over the tribe of his older brother, Manasseh.

The family, looking on at the time of the blessings given by Jacob, felt he had misplaced his hands. He had given the greater blessing to the younger. It was customary for the firstborn to receive the first and greater blessing.

We have no idea why the blessings were given in this way. Could the grandfather have been partial? Could the older boy have had a flaw in body or character? We do not know.

One thing all Christians must remember, God does not misplace His blessings.

We look at a family of children and say, "The middle boy is so nice looking, so friendly; he certainly will go far in the world."

God, looking at the same family, may give His blessings and His call to a completely different child. He sees into the heart, but we see only the outward appearance.

Remember the story of David, the shepherd lad, out on the hillside. His brothers were older and sturdier looking; yet God picked David for an important task.

As a child growing up I was taught never to question the decisions of my father. At times I could talk my mother into letting me do some desired project, my father never. Often in my heart I felt rebellious and angry. I thought my father just did not always know what was best.

As children of God, we must learn to abide by His decisions. My father was only human and I still think he was not always right. But our heavenly Father is always right. He is perfect and just. We may not understand His decisions at the time; but rest assured, they are right.

A few years ago ten men were trapped in a mine in West Virginia. The rescue workers, after a number of days, could get signals; so they knew some of the men were alive. The news reports told how the families of the trapped men waited at the mine entrance, each hoping their loved one would be found alive.

When at last the men were reached, four were dead and six alive. Four families were brokenhearted and six were rejoicing. How did God choose who would live and who would die?

The stories told how the first man to reach safety said, "Thank you, God."

All six men paused for prayer as they came to the entrance of the mine after almost ten days of being trapped in a tomb of darkness and death.

I do not know what the families of the four who were killed said. I know if I had been one of them I would have said, "Why, dear God, did it have to be my loved one taken?"

We never know why some are blessed more than others. Often, like Joseph, we are wondering if the hands of blessings have been misplaced.

One of the saddest things in life is to see a person whom God has blessed with a good mind, a strong body, and often a good education, yet with no purpose in life. That person has failed to recognize his great blessings and make the most of them.

How many times we read in the papers of some man or boy paralyzed from polio or an accident; yet that person by sheer grit and determination struggles to make a contribution to the world. And in the same city there will be a strong boy, full of promise, who wastes his life away by indulging in dope or alcohol.

It is not ours to question why God gave one boy a good body just to be squandered, while the paralyzed boy wants so much to bless the world.

When parents ask me questions about cases like this I can only quote Paul's inspired words, "For now we see through a glass, darkly; but then face to face: now I know in part; but then shall I know even as also I am known" (I Cor. 13:12).

I have three children and ten grandchildren. My only son lives six hundred miles away, across two states. My baby daughter lives in California, at least a two-days' drive away. My oldest daughter lives twenty-five miles from home. I could cry and carry on because they do not live in the same city with me. I could say that God has blessed my friend more abundantly, for she has three children, all living within walking distance of her home.

Why question the way life is arranged? Why not thank God that each child found a good life's companion and has an agreeable job? As long as my children are serving God and paying their tithe, I feel God will direct their lives so much better than I could even imagine.

God never misplaces His blessings. For we cannot see into the future, but He can. He knew why the shepherd lad, David, was best suited for the call He sent through the prophet Samuel.

He knew why Moses was the one suited for the call He made at the burning bush. He knows why His call went out to a tall, ungainly lad splitting wood, a lad who worked hard and became president of our great country.

What is our responsibility about God's blessings? We are to be submissive to His will and way. We are to be doers of the Word and not hearers only. As we accomplish one task, we will be stronger and more ready for harder ones.

THE GOOD THINGS

Life can be filled with such wonderful things:
Friendships and beauty with blossoms galore;
Love's inspiration that plucks the heart's strings;
Sunrise and sunset each day keeping score.

Home and dear loved ones, a bed for night's rest;
Labor at which we can earn what we need;
Food to sustain us in giving our best:
These are most wonderful blessings indeed!

Life's best possessions are seldom those things
Money alone with its power can buy;
Health and its blessings, the joy that it brings,
Are the sweet gift of the Father on high.

—J. T. Bolding

5

Style Show

And why take ye thought for raiment? Consider the lilies of the field, how they grow; they toil not, neither do they spin: And yet I say unto you, That even Solomon in all his glory was not arrayed like one of these. —Matthew 6:28, 29

Fall weather is in the air. We are thinking of what we will wear during the next months of cool and cold weather.

None of us want especially to look like clothes horses, but every woman wants to look attractive.

I once had a friend in a town where my husband was pastor. She always seemed to know just the right day or place when it would be appropriate to appear in public wearing a new outfit. She would look like a work of art on the first cold Sunday, when all the other women would appear in something dragged hastily out of storage.

Every line of her dress, coat, shoes, and purse would coordinate. She looked as if she just stepped off the plane from Paris.

Two women, of more than ample means, in our small city, would pay her to plan their costumes for them. Then they would try to look as perfect as she did.

People would often remark, "No matter what the season or occasion, she will be the best dressed woman in town."

In the same town I knew another woman, approximately the same age and financial and educational background. She bought very few clothes, but she was always trim. Her mind was on different achievements.

One day in a group of women who were spending their time gossiping, my chic friend was heard to remark, "If only S—— would buy some good clothes."

A listener came quickly to her defense: "She buys the best things in town; she is adorned with good works."

"Well, good works will not make her look very stylish at the yearly roundup of all the clubs in town," my friend replied.

The gossiping group were astonished when S——'s friend failed to drop the subject. Instead she quoted the following verses: "Strength and honour are her clothing; and she shall rejoice in time to come. She openeth her mouth with wisdom; and in her tongue is the law of kindness" (Prov. 31:25, 26).

For just a few moments I want you to think about what you will wear this fall.

Take out a dress from your closet and look at it. Look closely. It is getting old, isn't it? And almost every woman in town has one similar to it. The name of this garment is "fault-finding." Oh, please don't wear that dress, it looks ugly even on the fairest maiden. Discard it.

What will you wear in the place of this discarded garment? Here is one with the label "love thy neighbor." What a beautiful dress! This dress makes even the plainest woman look lovely. Be sure to wear this garment often.

Reach back in your closet. Perhaps you should discard some other garments.

Yes, there is a coat. It looks nice at first glance, but it is labeled "selfishness." No one wants to be around a selfish person long. That is certainly a coat you will want to discard.

Now here is a cloak labeled "the cloak of righteousness." This is an attractive coat. Why not wear it this fall?

But one dress is not going to be enough, even if it is labeled "love thy neighbor."

Here is one that looks rather unattractive as you take it out of the closet. It is labeled "sensitiveness." Now, what is wrong with this garment? Oh, I see; it needs to be made over. You wear it with a feeling of sensitiveness to all that people say about you. You really have a chip on your shoulder when wearing this dress. Make it over, take off the chip. Make this a dress with a feeling of sensitiveness for others' needs and desires. It will look lovely made over. In place of always seeing a slight or a hurt, you will be careful to make others feel wanted and accepted in your circle.

Now you have selected some lovely dresses, such as "love thy neighbor" and "consideration for others' feelings." You have a nice "cloak of righteousness" to wear over your dresses. We must select a pair of gloves which will match the dresses and cloak. How would this pair called "service" fit? Hands always look more beautiful when they wear the gloves of service.

Feet are very important if a woman wants to look neat and attractive. What kind of shoes will go with such good clothes? Ephesians 6:15 reads like this: "And your feet shod with the preparation of the gospel of peace."

How could feet fail to look nice when wearing the "preparation of peace"? Another verse in the Old Testament mentions beautiful feet, wearing these very same shoes: "How beautiful upon the mountains are the feet of him that bringeth good tidings, that publisheth peace; that bring good tidings of good, that publisheth salvation; that saith unto Zion, Thy God reigneth!"

All the clothes I have told you about today are such good buys. They will never wear out or look out of date. You will always feel well dressed and confident when wearing these garments.

At a style show several years ago I heard the narrator say, "No woman should step outside the house without her pearls on."

Well, today we are all for crocheted beads. We put them on early in the morning and wear them all day.

I think jewelry is very pleasing, for it adds a touch of glamor to any woman's costume. Yet today I would plead with all of you to obtain the pearl of great price—the salvation and love of Jesus Christ.

A very beautiful and wealthy woman, much indulged and loved by her husband, became ill and was on her deathbed. The husband was frantic. Seeking to show her his great love and concern, he bought a lovely and expensive brooch. Taking it to the hospital room, he pinned it on her gown. "Now you are the most expensively dressed woman in the hospital," he told her.

"You mean well," she whispered, "but I am going to die. I am going to a place where diamonds are worn only in a crown, and my crown is so empty."

As we think for a moment about what we are going to wear in our hearts and in our attitudes this fall, I want us to join together and sing the chorus of the old, old song: "Will There Be Any Stars?"

> *Will there be any stars, any stars in my crown,*
> *When at evening the sun goeth down?*
> *When I wake with the blest*
> *In the mansions of rest,*
> *Will there be any stars in my crown?*

(Close with a prayer for more dedicated lives.)

6

Look in All Directions

Thou shalt remember all the way which the Lord thy God hath led thee. —Deuteronomy 8:2

I was well pleased to have a letter from my college-age grand-daughter. She told me all about a trip she had made to spend a week-end with her boy friend on his parents' cattle ranch. The thing I liked the most about her very happy and enthusiastic report was this: at bedtime each evening the father called all the family into the family room and read a devotion and had prayer. I felt my granddaughter had chosen the right type of a boy for her friend.

When children hear Scripture read at home and are led to worship God, they will not stray too far from the right path.

Sometimes the young are terribly bored when older people tell stories about times past. In our Scripture, Moses is doing that very thing. He is recounting to the Hebrew people all the ways the Lord had led them.

How exciting the stories must have been when the older Hebrews told their children about the flight out of Egypt. How frightened they were with a sea of water in front of them and an army behind. Then God took charge!

Some of us grew up in an era when money and the things people buy with money were scarce. We had little of worldly goods; yet what do we remember about our childhood?

We remember the joyous, happy times. I remember my girlhood was spent in a town where many people—including my parents—kept a cow and some chickens. When I needed an extra dime I would often ask my mother for a gallon of buttermilk, or a dozen eggs. These I would take several blocks away to a poor section of town, going from door to door until someone wanted to buy. Don't pity me; this was great fun! I knew no fear. I was in no danger. People in our town had never heard of dope; and since we were living in an age of prohibition, we never saw an intoxicated person. I can't remember ever sleeping in a house with locked doors, until I had been married over ten years.

Moses wanted people to remember the good in the past, the power of the God who delivered them, and the fact that their God was still alive.

Like the Hebrews of old, we are God's children. Let us look in the direction our lives have traveled over the years, and see some of the great blessings of God. Let the goodness of God and the abundance of His mercies pass before you. Think of the bright, happy times, not of the depths of sorrow or despair.

When I was a little barefoot girl, walking in the hot east Texas sun with a gallon of milk in a syrup bucket with a lid clamped tightly on it, I enjoyed every moment of the walk. I knew the names of many of the children I met along the way, and most of the time they would walk along with me. We would talk of big things, like how many freight cars they counted in a long train that day. Or often we would plan to go rock hunting on the tracks, when my mother would allow me to visit them.

The way you look at the goodness and mercies of God makes the difference in whether you are a gloomy person or a smiling, happy one.

Can you remember in the days of the past when you sat on the bank of a river or creek and looked at the trees and clouds reflected in the water? But if you went very close and put your face down near the water, you could see mud and filth.

All of life depends on your way of looking at things. How grateful we should be as we remember all the ways which the Lord has led us.

You can look at life and see the mud and filth of a sin-filled world, or you can see reflected in those about you the glorious blessings of a God who loves His children.

When my husband was a young man he planned to attend the Southwestern Baptist Seminary at Fort Worth, Texas. In that day we believed that if we worked hard enough and prayed to be in God's will, He would take care of the rest. After saving every cent possible, we loaded our worldly goods into a trailer, put our three children in the car, and started for Fort Worth. Imagine our surprise when we arrived in Fort Worth and found that people did not want to rent apartments on Seminary Hill to a couple with three children. We had thought everyone would like our children. We did.

Nevertheless, God knew just where He planned for us to live. By the end of the day we were securely moved into a comfortable four-room apartment.

God had plans for us and that apartment. For, you see, on the other side of the house there was a small grocery store with living quarters behind for the man who owned the store. In less than two months that store belonged to us. I would work while my husband was in class, and he would work while I was in class. As soon as the old man had moved away to live with his children, a young minister asked to rent the living quarters behind the store. He was able to bring his wife and little girl to live with him.

Then my husband's sister came to help us work and to attend school part time. She fell in love with a young man who wanted very much to attend the seminary. They married and were able, because of the store, to go on to school. Today one of those preachers is president of the Arizona Baptist Convention. The other one is retiring this year after many years of very fruitful service in south Texas.

We are prone to look in only one direction—at the big problems of the moment. But God wants us to look three ways. Look backward at all His providential care. Be grateful for the past.

Then look forward. Paul said, "I press toward the mark, unto the prize of the high calling of God in Christ Jesus." Look forward to the things you want to accomplish for the glory of God.

You must have a purpose for your life, for your service. In some of our cities there are swarms of aimless young people, far away from home, often hungry and sick. Why are they there? They failed to look backward at the good in the world, they failed to look forward to what they could accomplish in life, so they drift aimlessly without purpose or goal.

You must not only look backward and forward in life, but you must look upward. Look unto Jesus, the author and the finisher of our faith. Do you face disappointments? Jesus knew them, also. Do you face poverty? Jesus knew that, too. Always keep looking above in prayer and Scripture reading, and you will find your spirit renewed each day.

Our California daughter and her family started home this past September after a three-week vacation. They were going by way of Four Corners down through the Indian country to Flagstaff. As they left the last trading post before the long drive into Flagstaff, rain began to come down in sheets. They were in real danger, for darkness came on early and there was no place to stop. In telling about it later, they said often a line in the center of the road was all they could go by. Sometimes the rain would let up for a few moments, and then they would speed ahead to make some headway.

Life is like that. Christ is always there to guide us if we will but keep our eye on Him. At times we can accomplish a lot; then we must slow down again for the trials and burdens of life.

LOOK TO YOUR LIGHT

Has someone seen Christ in you today?
Christian, look to your life, I pray.
There are aching and blighted souls
Being lost on sin's destructive shoals,
And perhaps of Christ their only view
May be what of Him they see in you.
Will they see enough to bring hope or cheer?
Look to your light—does it shine out clear?
                                        —Unknown

7

Hit-and-Run Christians

And Jesus said unto him, No man, having put his hand to the plough, and looking back, is fit for the kingdom of God. —Luke 9:62

The headlines glared out at us at the breakfast table. "Hit-and-run driver kills one and leaves one critically injured."

How could he have been so cruel? our whole city asked.

Two teen-aged boys, working at a night job, were going home on their new motor bike. It was the first night they had ridden it to work. A careless driver smashed into them and sped away into the darkness.

The boy who lived was able to describe the car, and in a few days the offender was caught. He was not much older than the boys he had run into.

"Why didn't you stop and help?" the judge asked at his trial.

"I had never been in any kind of accident before and I was afraid. I didn't think they would find me. I didn't want to be involved. My dad would take my car away from me."

Not much defense for driving away and leaving one dead boy and one so seriously injured he would have died if help had not come by quickly.

Our churches are literally filled (or should I say the rolls are filled) with hit-and-run Christians. Those are the members who are present each service if some big out-of-town minister is holding services. They piously go to the front and tell the speaker how wonderful he is. They even take time to tell him a few of the things that are so wrong in their own church. Then when the visitor is gone they go home and do not return to services until Easter or some other special day comes along. In other words, they hit the popular services, disappear, and come back when it pleases them.

On the other hand, there is the hit-and-run Christian who always comes at the first of a church year. He makes a big pledge and takes a class or other position of importance. This type of Christian is well able to pay the pledge; he is capable of teaching a class; but, after all, the second month of the new year is not all that exciting. No one is coming around to say what a wonderful fellow he is to pledge this much or to teach this class.

He becomes angry; he panics. He doesn't really want to be involved; so he quits! He cancels his pledge because they are not spending the money in the manner he feels is best.

Read Scripture to see what Jesus said about hit-and-run Christians. In John 6:66, 67 we read, "From that time many of his disciples went back, and walked no more with him. Then said Jesus unto the twelve, Will ye also go away?"

How sad our Lord must be today as He looks at the sinful and needy world and sees so many hit-and-run Christians. Very often He must be saying, "Will ye also go away?"

Thank God for the ones who stay true and faithful in times of excitement and in times of calm and plodding progress.

My favorite person, my husband, often says, "God's work goes forward on willing shoulders."

A few years ago a man ran over a child while he was driving to work down the main street in our city. The man was in no way at fault. The child was running carelessly from an older sister, not even stopping to look for danger. She just darted out in front of the car.

The man stopped. He called an ambulance and sent for the child's mother. For weeks the man spent money, time, and effort trying to help the child get well again.

That man typifies a patient Christian. He is one who is not to blame for the careless sin of the unsaved; yet he is willing to go on, far past the call of duty in order to win that person, in order to see a man or woman healed of the terrible disease of sin.

Most churches rotate the men who act as ushers. It is surprising that some are so faithful in their service. There was one man in our church who was never absent from his duties. He was always kind and efficient. When the new year started, a new set of ushers was assigned. Suddenly this man and his wife stopped coming to church. When asked the reason, they replied, "They fired me from my job."

They never took the trouble to find out that the policy of the church was to use different men each year in order to train more men in service. They never bothered to volunteer for some quiet task that would have no glamor.

There are some people who have hit-and-run dispositions. They are off again-on again about everything in life.

The greatest of missionaries once said, "Be ye stedfast, unmoveable, always abounding in the work of the Lord" (I Cor. 15:58).

Betty and Alice were best friends at school. One day the teacher announced that a special program would be held after school. Each child must have a twenty-five cent admission fee, in order to attend the program.

Betty and Alice counted their money. Betty had a dime, and Alice had a nickle. They couldn't go because they did not have enough money.

"I'll ask the teacher if I can get in if you give me your nickle," Betty told her friend.

"No, you must have twenty-five cents," the teacher said.

Many people want to get into the kingdom of heaven by borrowing all they can from friends and family for their admission fee. That will not work! You must be born again. You must accept Christ fully and with your whole life, or fail completely. Betty and Alice were just as far from getting into the show with their dime and nickle as they would have been with no money at all.

Christ did not approach the cross, then run away when He saw how horrible it was going to be. As would-be followers, we must surrender all to Him or be lost.

THE GOOD TALK

There are many today who will talk a good game,
  But their lives fail to bear out their speech,
And the minds of their friends often question the same
  When it's seen they live not as they teach.

There are many who sing their own praises so long
  They make some think they have to be great;
But it's soon very clear, they are not worth the song
  And you class them below second rate.

Oh, for genuine character that is for real;
  Oh, for people whose word will stand true,
And for lives full of zeal whose true worth you can feel;
  For you know what they say, they will do.

—J. T. Bolding

8

Sincerely Yours

The grace of our Lord Jesus Christ be with you all. Amen. —Revelation 22:21

To the only wise God our Saviour, be glory and majesty, dominion and power, both now and ever. Amen. —Jude 25

During World War II I lived across the alley from a Methodist minister's wife. She was to me the very essence of Christianity. There I was, alone in a strange little town. I had the responsibility of taking care of my three children while my husband was serving as a chaplain overseas.

There she was, living in a comfortable parsonage, her husband a popular pastor, and, seemingly, her world secure.

She was much nicer to me than any of my own denomination I met in that town. After her husband was transferred to another church, we began to correspond.

A few months after my own world was made right again and we were a whole family once more, she wrote her last letter. Oh, what a sad letter it was; for she was dying of the dread disease leukemia. She ended her letter, "I will see you when we meet again in heaven."

In our wonderful Bible we have a number of letters which close with the words: "The grace of our Lord Jesus Christ be with you all." It seems fitting that John closed the very last book of the Bible with those words.

When I was a teen-ager, a popular way to close a letter (to the right person) was with kisses. And we would make all kinds of X's. Don't laugh—if you've never received a letter with kisses from your best boy friend or girl friend, you just haven't lived. Of course, in this present day of promiscuity youth may not get excitement from such a pastime.

As a mother, I always sign my letters to the children with some type of love words.

In Acts 1:8, we have the last words Jesus spoke to His followers. They were a promise of power to come to them through the Holy Spirit.

There are many ways to say, "Sincerely yours." A dedicated child of God says this in the way he seeks to help and win others.

I have always been impressed with the selfless dedication of the Wycliffe translators. I happen to know two personally, but I want to tell you about one I have only heard about.

Miss Viola Griste was a translator in a remote village in Mexico, working with an Indian tribe. In this tribe she found a small girl named Elna who was born without any ears. Where ears should have been, there was not even an opening.

Miss Griste brought Elna to Oklahoma City. There a very fine ear surgeon offered his skill to help the child. After his operation and some time of treatment, Elna could hear. To hear meant she could learn to talk. Her life was now becoming exciting, for she now had the one thing she had longed for. Ears!

Other seven-year-old girls in her village wore their long hair pulled back from their ears, but not Elna. Now she could not only hear and talk, but she no longer had any reason to be ashamed of a head without any ears. A firm in California made her some plastic ears; so at last she felt like a whole person and was happy.

How are we saying, "Sincerely yours" to those about us? So many people say to the world, "Sincerely yours," but they do not mean it.

They shut themselves off from doing good and spend their days with trivial things. They think petty thoughts, and as a consequence they leave no sweet memory of their lives in the hearts of others.

When we send a business letter we usually sign it in a standard fashion. Sometimes if we are urgent about a matter we will say: "Hoping to hear from you soon."

Everyday we forget to pray, our heavenly Father must long to hear from us soon. Each opportunity we pass by and fail to witness for Christ must make God feel we are not sincere when we say, "Sincerely yours."

The way we sign our letters often tells what relationship we have with the one we are writing to. Likewise, the way we live our lives often shows what relationship we have with the Giver of life.

A few years ago, in Monticello, Indiana, a boy proved how much he loved his mother. He was just an ordinary, fun-loving boy. His mother had pleased him so much by becoming a den mother for his Cub Scout group. One day he was all dressed in his uniform, waiting for the rest of the boys to come to the pack meeting.

A man came to the house with a gun and started to shoot his mother. Sammy Joe jumped in front of his mother and was shot in the head. He loved his mother enough to try a desperate move to save her life.

I do not know whether the mother lived or died, for she was also shot a moment later, but I know her little son said in a language the world understands, "I love you, mother."

Do we by our actions say to our world, "I love You, Jesus my Lord. I will die for You if I need to"?

Looking at an animal picture on television one night, I saw an ostrich taking a drink of water. After the bird took a drink, he raised his long throat and pointed his mouth toward the sky. "What a long way the water has to travel to reach his stomach," I observed. Then I thought, "He may be raising his head to thank God for his drink."

How often we greet a friend after a long separation, "Why didn't you write?"

"Oh, I just am not much at letter writing," the friend may apologize.

The letter of life we are composing is one we set forth regardless of how well or how poorly we write.

We can wish for others the best in life, we can take an interest, lend a helping hand, make each day worthwhile, or we can merely fill our pages with scribbles. Your life is a letter, long or short. You are the one who will choose much of what goes in that letter.

BEAUTY

There is beauty all around us,
  Which some blindly never see;
In some form it's ever ready
  To bless folk like you and me.

You may see it in the sunset,
  Dewy grass, and sunrise too;
Lovely gardens, forests, twilight,
  And bright stars through skies so blue;

Show'rs of rain and gorgeous flowers;
  Orchards, meadows, fruitful fields;
But the beauty that's the greatest
  Is the kind the good life yields:

Loving kindness, tender mercy,
  Christ-like homes so rich and rare;
Thoughtfulness which always blesses,
  From the heart of those who care.

These, plus friendship, sweet, enduring,
  Overflowing from your life,
Make a paradise of beauty
  Here amid this world of strife.

—J. T. Bolding

9
Shut the Door!

But thou, when thou prayest, enter into thy closet, and when thou hast shut thy door, pray to thy Father which is in secret; and thy Father which seeth in secret shall reward thee openly. —Matthew 6:6

One cold winter Saturday my children were restless and resented having to stay inside. Every few moments I found myself calling out, "Shut the door!" For they were going to the door and opening it to see if the weather was really as cold as I told them.

At last I said, "Shut the door and listen." Then I gave a few motherly instructions about putting on warm clothes and told them to go outside but to keep the door shut.

Today my children are gone and have children of their own to care for. Often I think how nice it would be to have a little one opening the door and peeping out.

The children of God never get too old for Him to say, "Shut the door and listen."

How many sorrows and mistakes would be avoided if we had only shut the door and listened—listened to the will and direction of our heavenly Father.

Like our children, we so often hear all the calls and demands of the outside world. It seems to us we just can't take time to "shut the door and listen."

A young woman was deeply in love. Before the time for her wedding, the young man was called into service and sent across the country. Her heart was broken. She felt he would be years getting out of service, and she was afraid he might find someone he liked better in the distant city.

One day he sent her a letter and asked her to call him at a certain number on a certain day and hour. She was so happy at the thought of getting to talk to her lover. She did not want to call from her home, so she went to a public phone booth.

Her connection was made, and her sweetheart eagerly answered. She could not hear clearly his words of love and endearment. When she complained to him she could not hear, he replied, "Shut the door of the phone booth." When the door was closed she could hear clearly, and she felt happy and secure in the words she heard.

In our modern world it is hard to shut the door on the radio, the television, the neighbors. Yet if we would talk and commune with God, we must close the door to the outside noises.

When we go aside and close the door to all but God we feel a divine nearness.

We receive help for the solutions to our problems.

We get strength for enduring our infirmities.

We receive mercy and forgiveness for our mistakes.

We find deliverance from our troubles.

Best of all, we feel a renewed filling of the Holy Spirit.

It is hard to find a quiet place to close the door and listen to God.

A family of six children living in a farm home with only four rooms might be said to have lots of togetherness. Yet the children all knew they were not to talk or make noise at bedtime while each knelt for private prayers.

How sad and even inexcusable, that with spacious homes and private rooms, many people find it hard to get enough quiet from the everyday noises to talk to God.

One man was disturbed over a business problem. He had the opportunity to vote yes or no on the issue in his organization. If he said yes, he would make a lot of money. If he voted no, a lot of stockholders would not lose the money they had invested.

Being a Christian, he truly wanted to say no. But his associates pressured him to vote yes. At last the night before the vote was to be taken, he went to the country to be alone and think. He found himself near a cemetery. He parked and started walking.

He thought no one in the city of the dead would try to talk back to him or influence him in any way. As he walked about, pondering and talking to himself about his problem, he saw printed on a headstone, "He put his treasures in heaven." Another place he saw the words, "She lived to serve." He became so fascinated with the different inscriptions that he stopped thinking about his problem and just started reading.

Suddenly a disturbing thought—or was it God speaking—came to the man: Would a true inscription on his tombstone have to be, "Here lies one who cheated the small stockholder in order to make himself richer"?

The man sighed, "Oh, God, I just needed to talk to You again. I want to do the right thing."

His partners never could understand his decision, but the only answer he gave was, "I want to live and act like a Christian."

If you want a powerful life, in any phase, you must lead a prayerful life. The person who never prays is a person without his full potential of power. Of course, in order to pray to God, you must first know Him.

When I was a girl in college I just could not work my algebra and trig problems. A boy named Tom could not write his English themes. We often worked together, helping each other. He made my problems come out so well with the right answer.

Today when I have some problems which seem unanswerable, I go to the Friend of all friends. When we close the door on the world and say, "Here, Lord, are my problems. I can't solve them, but I know you can give me the answer," we find serenity as well as wisdom.

After the war in 1946, shoes were scarce. A man in Japan had secured at much cost and sacrifice a nice pair of shoes. He was so proud of his possession that he would go about looking at his feet.

Then one day he was invited to hear a famous man speak at a local church. He wanted so much to go, but he was afraid to attend the meeting. The custom was to take off one's shoes and leave them outside the door. "Who will watch my shoes if I go?"

His friend wanted him to go so much; so he thought a moment, then replied, "God will watch your shoes."

So many of us today long for communion with God; but we are so possessed with worldly problems we keep asking, "Who will watch our shoes?"

Just put your shoes aside and shut the door. In a quiet moment with God, you will forget worldly problems and find true riches.

If you really want to listen to the sounds of nature, it is wise to go far away into the wilderness and halt all activity. We were reminded of this one Sunday morning on a vacation trip along the East Coast. We had decided to go to church in Concord; so we left our motel early and drove along toward that city. As we drove there we saw a small sign which read "Walden Pond."

"Oh, we must see that. We almost missed it," my husband remarked as he parked the car.

We started walking in the direction of the arrow. After a short time we found ourselves in a thickly wooded area. If there had not been a footpath, we would have been lost.

When we came to the pond, we realized it would be called a giant lake in west Texas. We stook silently in wonder at the beauty around us.

Not another person was anywhere in view. We were so impressed, we caught ourselves talking in whispers. It was as if we were in a heavenly place and wanted to be reverent.

For a few moments we were so preoccupied with the glory and wonder of God's creation that we felt an urge to utter a prayer of thanksgiving to our God for allowing us to be there.

We had to leave in order to attend the church service. The service was pleasant and the people friendly, but the highlight of our day had been the early morning quiet as we looked at Walden Pond.

PROBLEMS

The problems in arithmetic,
  All planned out in the book,
Are often such a lot of fun;
  But try a meal to cook.

The answers in arithmetic,
  To check you only look
And you will find them in the book;
  But try a fish to hook.

You do things in arithmetic
  By rule, in every nook,
And sure, you'll get the answer but
  Just try to catch a crook.

It's fun to do arithmetic
  With answers in the book;
Life's problems may so different be:
  You must stop, listen, and look.

—J. T. Bolding

10

Live Today

Take therefore no thought for the morrow: for the morrow shall take thought for the things of itself. Sufficient unto the day is the evil thereof. —Matthew 6:34

How much less anxiety we would have if we could just trust our Lord and live each day as it comes.

A man from the city went to a lake in the South for some much-needed rest and relaxation. He hired a guide with a boat to take him out on the lake for some fishing. Out on the lake the man kept worrying about how the guide was steering the boat.

Finally the guide said, "Mister, you came here to fish. Now why don't you fish and let me steer the boat?

How often our Father in heaven must long for us to relax and live, while He steers the boat.

In the sunroom of an old folks' home three elderly women were talking to a visiting minister.

"I've had lots of troubles in my life," said one. "I've spent sleepless nights over them. But the ones that worried me most never happened."

"My old man," said one chuckling, "used to tell me I carried around three bags of problems all the time. Those I really had, those I used to have, and those I expected to have tomorrow."

The third lady looked at the vigorous young minister. "Right now I can't seem to remember my troubles. The Lord told me to cast all my cares on Him, and He always helped me over the hard places. Thank Him each night for the good of the day and forget the bad."

The young minister said good-bye and went about his duties. He was facing a perplexing problem when he had entered the home. He still faced the problem, but he said as he went about, "He will help me over the hard places."

Those women had very little future to look forward to; yet they were remembering the good things from the past.

It is never wise to look back at problems. Forget them. Live today!

A couple were invited to attend a small elite meeting of some of their dearest college friends. They all had been out of college twenty-one years. The host and hostess called it a "coming-of-age" party.

Six couples met on the specified day in the palatial home of one couple. They had grown very rich. They had sent their private plane to pick up those living farthest away.

One couple was in full-time Christian service. They felt embarrassed at their badly scuffed luggage, but forgot it in the joy of seeing their old college pals.

Sitting around the table at noon, it seemed each couple had so much to tell about their children and their fine homes.

"What kind of a home do you two religious fanatics have?" Linda asked. She had always owned a sharp tongue, but most of the others put up with her because they liked her husband so well.

"Well, Linda," the religious worker replied, "we are paying on a mansion. We never expect to miss a payment or to have a foreclosure. It is so beautiful it defies description. Our architect is the greatest, and we are leaving everything to His choice."

"Oh, I thought you two were very poor. Why didn't you ask us to your mansion?" Linda said.

"You can visit our mansion only by trusting Christ and living a life for Him. We would so much like to know you will all be there some day."

There was a quiet over the crowd for a moment; then someone told a funny incident and the reunion went on. But at least one or two in the group wondered if they were spending too much effort on worldly things and not enough on the service their friend talked about. At least none dared to pity him again.

As the plane winged its way back to the distant city where a mission with many problems awaited, Jenny said to her husband, "Poor Linda, the wheels of her brain are so greased with greed she will never know the peace and happiness we enjoy."

"Thank you, dear, for feeling that way. I wish I could have told them I had furnished you more comforts here."

"Oh, dear, but we are so happy. I wouldn't want to be as bitter as Linda seemed." She snuggled up to her husband and thought of all the exciting things she would have to tell the children when they arrived home.

We are not storerooms, but channels;
We are not cisterns, but springs;
Passing our benefits onward,
Fitting our blessings with wings;
Letting the water flow outward
To spread o'er the desert forlorn;
Sharing our bread with our brothers,
Our comfort with those who mourn.
—Unknown

A Christian should memorize three verses of Scripture and always keep them handy. All people have problems, but some solve them easier than others.

The first verse to remember and quote is Ephesians 5:20, "Giving thanks always for all things unto God and the Father in the name of our Lord Jesus Christ."

A friend called one night to tell us about her broken heart. Her only son had told her that day he was suing his wife for divorce.

We quoted this verse to her, although I wondered how she could give thanks for a broken home.

Early next morning our friend called on the phone. "I have been giving thanks all night to God. I am so glad our son married and has a precious little boy. Now what do I do?"

"Now you must memorize another verse and quote it to yourself as you face these problems. This is a very short statement: I Thessalonians 5:16: "Rejoice evermore.""

The woman could not keep her son from breaking up his home, but she could be thankful for the small grandson she had as a result of the marriage. She could rejoice in the health and happiness of the child, and she could pray for the parents.

After we talked, I told her about another verse I felt she should practice. It is Ephesians 4:32: "And be ye kind one to another, tenderhearted, forgiving one another, even as God for Christ's sake hath forgiven you."

If you will remember always to look for the things you have to be thankful for, regardless of the situation, then you will be able to rejoice. As long as you have life, you have something to be thankful for and rejoice about.

Our problems are usually brought about by our contact or involvement with other people. We must remember to be kind to others if we would be happy.

How can you be kind to someone who has been unkind to you? Tell them about your Lord and Savior Jesus Christ.

LIVE TODAY

Tomorrow I'll forget today:
Its dreary fog and gloom;
For then the sun will chase the gray
And flowers again will bloom.

Tomorrow I'll forget today:
Its problems and its woe;
So why upset and fret my way
As through these hours I go?

I note that yesterday is past:
It will not come again,

But precious memories that last
Are never lived in vain.

Today is really all that's mine:
Its moments, one by one;
And so I'll help the sun to shine
For others till it's done.

I have decided just to live
My life from day to day,
And to each moment try to give
My very best alway.

—J. T. Bolding

11

Fasten Your Seat Belts

And what I say unto you I say unto all, Watch. —Mark 13:37

Watch ye therefore, and pray always, that ye may be accounted worthy to escape all these things that shall come to pass, and to stand before the Son of man. —Luke 21:36

In February of 1972, the news came out of Tehran, Iran, that at least six thousand villagers had been killed in a blizzard that dumped as much as twenty-six inches of snow on a section of country. This same country had been suffering from drought for four years.

Visitors were there from other countries, having a holiday climbing on the mountains. No one believed there could be such a life-destroying snow; so no one left.

On August 25, 1618, a man came to the village of Pleuers. The town was very prosperous, built on rich ground at the foot of a mountain. The man warned all the people in the village about a large cleavage in the mountain. He was convinced it was breaking open and would destroy the town.

All the people laughed at the man. Finally his only daughter agreed to leave with him. As they hurried away from the town she appealed to her father to wait for her in a safe place while she went back to lock her house door.

While she was back in her house the mountain did fall and all the people were killed. The man could only say over and over, "I tried to warn them!"

All along our highways we pass signs saying "Fasten Seat Belts." Yet we often travel hundreds of miles without ever putting the seat belt around us.

A father, mother, and two children were taking a long trip. Each time they saw the sign "Fasten Seat Belts" they would laugh and say, "We will later; it's too hot now."

Then they came upon a bad wreck. A large transport truck had gone out of control and ran into a car, killing several people.

When they were finally allowed to pass, each member of the family silently fastened his seat belt.

As Jesus talked to His disciples, He gave them this warning: "Watch ye therefore, and pray always, that ye may be accounted worthy to escape all these things that shall come to pass, and to stand before the Son of man" (Luke 21:36).

This warning is not from a mere man who sees trouble in the future, it is from our divine Lord. Yet how often we say, "I'll watch and get ready later in life." Life grows later each moment you live. There may not be time to go back for a useless treasure. God may come today.

Highway departments do not go to the trouble of putting up signs for safety measures just for fun. They know there is a real danger.

God didn't give us a Book that tells us to watch and pray simply because He knew it would be a best seller. He knows the day and hour you will be called to meet Him. You know that you must be ready at all times.

> *Life is real! Life is earnest!*
> *And the grave is not its goal:*
> *"Dust thou art, to dust returnest,"*
> *Was not spoken of the soul.*
>
> —Longfellow

Now is the time to fasten your seat belt and be prepared for the wrecks and problems that life will send your way.

As I grow older I realize my body is wearing out. I require more rest just to keep doing the essential things required of me. Oh, how safe it feels to know that even though my body may soon be dust, my soul will soar away to places prepared by my Lord and Savior.

As you rush about your daily pursuits, take time to check your seat belt. Are you fully committed to Christ? Are you safe in His love?

"Boast not thyself of tomorrow, for thou knowest not what a day may bring forth" (Prov. 27:1).

A popular Bible teacher in Dallas, Texas, during the early 1900s was J. B. Cranfill. He often said to his very large class, "Let us live every day as if it were the last."

I attended many funerals during and after World War II. At the military funerals they always played taps.

> *Day is done!*
> *Gone the sun!*
> *From the hill, from the lake, from the sky.*
> *All is well!*
> *Safely rest.*
> *God is nigh!*

Often my heart ached with sadness, for I knew that some of the soldiers buried with military honors were not really prepared to meet God. They had put off getting ready until it was too late.

A mother and father became parents again in their middle years, and in their joy became overly lenient in disciplining their little son. Their older children, grown and married, would often say, "You wouldn't let us act like that."

"Oh, he is so little and cute now. We will be stricter later."

But later was too late. The boy at sixteen stayed out of school so much he missed his promotion one year. He was in trouble with the law at eighteen; and the parents, too late, could see they should have been firm all along.

Time is of greatest importance. Once it is gone, we cannot call it back. Once a character is molded and formed, it is very hard to change it.

A girl came to us with a broken heart because her father's estate was not divided as she felt it should have been. "We talked about how much he needed to make a will, but none of us had the courage to mention it. He died suddenly, and so his estate was settled by a court."

How often this story is told over and over. People should make a will which will provide for their loved ones, but many feel the making of a will can be put off.

There is no time to waste. We must trust our lives to One who loved us—loved us enough to come to earth and die for our atonement. Today is the day of salvation.

HE HAS PURCHASED MY RELEASE

Tomorrow may some sorrow bring
To injure me with its sting,
And crush my spirit with its load
Of poisoning sin along my road;

But by His grace I know the peace
Of trusting in my God's release
From sin and death and their curse—
Tho Satan's demons do their worst.

Our Lord has promised in His book
To succor those who will look—
Like trusting children—in His Grace
And wait for Him with upturned face.

So when great sorrows bend me low
As through this life I onward go,
My inward joy shall never cease,
For he has purchased my release.

                              —Edward V. Wood

*Used by permission of Mr. Wood from his book *Poetic Thoughts of a Business Man.*

12
Stand in the Wind

He sendeth out his word, and melteth them: he causeth his wind to blow, and the waters flow. —Psalm 147:18

And suddenly there came a sound from heaven as of a rushing mighty wind, and it filled all the house where they were sitting. —Acts 2:2

We fear the elements of nature because we have no control over them. In a few moments' time a wind in the form of a cyclone can tear a city to pieces. People living on the coast of Florida fear the hurricane winds. Yet there are some wonderful and useful advantages to the wind.

On a trip from Fort Worth to Lubbock, Texas, we came to a very barren stretch of country. There were no houses for miles around. The land on either side of the road for many miles belongs to a big ranching company known as 6666.

We saw a number of windmills that were just standing idle.

"Why aren't they going?" I asked. "The wind is strong today."

"There is a chain which fastens the windmill in a still position. The chain must be released if the wind is to blow them."

Then we came to a windmill that was going very fast. Water was coming from the pipe and cattle were gathered around the tank, drinking contentedly.

How like a Christian, I thought. So many sit idle day after day, never feeling the power of God's Holy Spirit moving them. Then we meet a Christian turned on for God. He is busy working to bring in the kingdom.

What a great amount of spiritual power could be turned loose to help the world, if Christians would only stand in the wind of the Holy Spirit and take the restraining chains of sin off their lives.

Ministers often wonder why great crowds of people go to one church and very few to another. They should take a lesson from the windmills. No cattle went to drink at the mills which were not running. The cattle went to drink where the mill was being blown fiercely by the wind and water was gushing out.

People go to hear the man who is standing in the wind and letting the Holy Spirit use him for God.

Every born-again Christian has much unused power—power just waiting for us if we will stand in the wind of the Holy Spirit and be willing to be used. We can do mighty works for God if we only turn loose our inhibitions and stand ready for the power.

Our Scripture says, "He causeth his wind to blow."

We cannot just sit down and say, "Here I am, Holy Spirit. Come and make me a great gushing well sending forth the living water."

A windmill, if it is to pump water when the wind blows against its blades, must first meet some conditions. There must be a pipe going from the windmill on top of the earth deep down into the ground where there is an underground stream of water.

How can a person stand in the wind of the Holy Spirit unless that person had a deep and abiding love for Christ as his Lord and Savior?

One of my friends has a miniature windmill in her backyard. It is eight feet tall, painted silver and red. Very pretty. She says her grandchildren like to watch the blades go around, but it never brings any water from the earth. It has no pipe going into the ground and connecting with a stream of water.

You may look like a genuine and fruitful Christian, you may seem to be standing in the wind of the Holy Spirit, but unless you are a child of the King you will never bring forth fruit for the Master.

The same wind that blows a windmill and brings water from the ground, can blow on a person sitting under a tree on a hot summer day and make him cool. The same wind can blow against a car traveling fast and make it go on less gasoline. The same wind can dry a line full of wet wash in a few moments. Likewise, not all people willing to stand in the will of God will be affected in the same manner.

I Corinthians 12:1-11 gives some different fruits or results of a Spirit filled life.

Some are given words of wisdom, some words of knowledge. To some the Spirit gives great faith, to some gifts of healing. To another the working of miracles; to another prophecy; to another discerning of spirits. But all gifts come from the same Spirit.

In verse 7 we are told that every "manifestation of the Spirit is given to every man to profit withal."

In whichever way the Lord should lead you, stand in the wind. Let your life be used with the talents you have.

Set no limitations on the good you are capable of accomplishing. Just turn your life over to the Spirit, and see what great and mighty things will be accomplished.

Activity without the Holy Spirit is like the toy windmill with no pipe going into the water source under the ground. It is futile.

A young man growing up on a ranch did not want to go to college. He loved ranch life and wanted to stay home. His pastor talked with him and encouraged him to attend a small college near his home. He was needed on the football team.

"I do not want to go, but I will pray about it. If it seems to be the will of God for me to go, I will," the boy told his pastor.

After much prayer and talking to his parents, the boy was still undecided. Just one week before school started he was at the windmill in the pasture, the wind was blowing and the water was coming out of the pipe, sweet and cool.

"Lord, here I stand. I love my life here, but use me like I use this old windmill. Turn me off or on as You see fit. I am Yours." The boy turned to his horse, and the horse without any urging started toward the ranch house. At the house, Peanuts, as he was affectionately called, said to his mother: "There must be some reason why I feel led to go to that college. I hate to study, but today I feel I must go."

At the small college, Peanuts was placed on the football team. He soon became amazed at the morals and language of some of the boys. He picked out the captain of the team to pray for. Soon he won that captain to Christ. Then together they started praying for another team member. On through a very successful season of winning games, Peanuts was winning lost boys to Christ. He was very popular with the whole school. Once he invited all the team to his home for a weekend. They stayed in the bunk house and ate ranch food prepared by the cook. On Sunday he took all the boys to the little village church.

To some people, this story has a sad ending. To Peanuts it was a happy one. During his sophomore year Peanuts became incurably ill. The doctors advised him to go home to the ranch and spend his last months in quiet.

He called the football squad together and told them he would be leaving. "I know now why the Lord sent me here. I am leaving you to win others in my place. I want so much to live, but I can't. So carry on for God and for the school."

During his remaining days he often talked to his parents and told them about the boys he had met at school. He was happy, knowing he had opened a better way of life for his friends, as well as the door to eternal life for those who had accepted Christ as Savior.

Christ gives us the will to serve Him; then He gives us the power.

NATURE

Brilliant hued cumulus clouds in the sunset,
  Sail-driven boats on a green bordered lake,
Healthy, fat cattle contentedly grazing
  Nullify ideas that life is a fake.

Rugged high mountains adorning horizons,
  Giant old redwoods that reach for the blue,
Wind-driven waves of rich grain on the prairie
  Keep the heart sure there's so much that is true.

Bright-colored birds flitting through the dense forest,
  Mockingbird songs overflowing with joy,

Playful wild creatures, free frolicking antics
Bring back the faith of a starry-eyed boy.

Winter-formed snow scenes of rare pristine beauty,
Thoughts returned godward again and again,
Earth's wondrous beauties will play on the heartstrings,
Nature's a marvelous builder of men.

—J. T. Bolding

13

Pay the Postage

Think not that I am come to destroy the law, or the prophets: I am not come to destroy, but to fulfil. —Matthew 5:17

One day when I was very busy my door bell rang. Going to the door, I found the postman. "You will have to pay one cent postage on this letter."

I paid the penny and went back to my work grumbling. "Why bother anyone for one penny?"

Then I remembered a story I had heard about a big ship that had sunk off shore. Through the years, people had gone out to see the ship all day long, gradually carrying in much sand on their shoes. The sand had slowly accumulated, so that at last the ship had so much sand on it that it sank.

Just a silly story; and yet if I had said people carried so many rocks into the ship it sank, you would have believed me.

If the postman had said I owed five or ten cents I would have paid and thought nothing about it. Yet if he has two hundred customers and all owed him one cent, he would eventually be losing a lot of money.

This is the attitude we take about sin in our lives. If it is just a small transgression, why bother with it. Yet the One who collects for big sins will also collect for the small.

I often think of something I would like to send my daughter in California. Many times I do not send the article because I do not want to pay such high postage.

Sin is like postage. We must pay postage on the sins we commit—the small as well as the great.

At the post office the postmaster has a chart he uses as a guide to tell him how much each package or letter will cost to mail.

God gave to Moses the Ten Commandments for a guide to His people. They are very brief; yet they express a connection between morality and religion. In other words, if we are followers of God, we will want to have a right relationship to our fellow men.

In His Sermon on the Mount Jesus talked to His followers about their relationship to others in the world.

Many people want God's grace, they want eternal life, but they do not want to pay the postage. They want everything for their convenience but give nothing in return.

God gave us the law through Moses and He gave us grace and truth through Jesus Christ; yet we should respond to both the same way. We should want to live by the commandments as nearly as we can. Above all, if we believe on Jesus, we will want to live by the great commandment of love He gave us.

Two boys discovered that an old woman lived in a large house alone. They started throwing their ball over her high board fence. Then they would climb over the fence and after retrieving the ball, would fill their pockets with fruit off the trees.

The old woman was past ninety and could not get to the door very fast. After the boys gathered fruit they would tear up the flowers and sometimes throw ripe fruit at the house.

The woman called out to them and asked them to stay out of her yard. They only laughed and said ugly things.

Then one day when peaches were ripe and very tempting, the boys came into the yard. They sat down to enjoy all the peaches they could eat.

The woman's son was visiting her that day. He phoned the police and asked them to come down the alley and catch the boys before they could run away.

Just as the boys finished eating and started throwing overripe fruit at the house, the back gate opened and there stood a huge policeman. He took the boys to the police station. They were thoroughly frightened, for they knew it was wrong to torment an old and helpless person.

It is man's nature to be perverse and willful, but it is God's nature to forgive us if we repent and ask for forgiveness.

My daughter was treasurer for her little club in school. Their whole sum of money consisted of thirty-five cents. She took good care of the money. Then one day she decided to take it to school and to the club meeting after school.

When school was out she reached far back in her desk to get her little purse, but the purse was gone. She was so disturbed. The teacher helped her look for the purse. They found it, empty, stuffed behind a radiator. At the club meeting the members were cross with her.

"You knew we were going to get a gift for our teacher with that money," they complained.

Later, at home when she told me her problem, I felt sad at her distress and gladly gave her the thirty-five cents to pay her debt.

All sin and transgression must be paid for. I know I am so sinful I could never pay for all the sins I commit. God felt sad at the condition of mankind. He sent His Son to die for us and pay our debt in full if we will only accept His salvation.

Yes, the postman must be paid. All things cost something. Sin costs in punishment; friendship costs in time and effort; love costs in sacrifice. We are our brother's keepers. We are not free just to take and take without ever giving in return.

PRAYING HEARTS

The "Praying Hands" are famous ones
Among the sculptured arts;
They symbolize what's needed most:
Strong, humble, praying hearts.

Of course they're just a symbol of
The kind of hearts we need
And what they're representing is
Our love in word and deed:

Our hearts bowed down in gratitude,
Our lives in God's dear hand,
All dedicated to his love,
To heed his wise command.

—J. T. Bolding

14
Gifts

A gift is as a precious stone in the eyes of him that hath it. —**Proverbs 17:8**

For the wages of sin is death; but the gift of God is eternal life through Jesus Christ our Lord. —**Romans 6:23**

Every man hath his proper gift of God, one after this manner, and another after that. —**I Corinthians 7:7**

At a convention I went into the ladies' lounge during a recess. Many women were milling around. Some were repairing their makeup, some just resting on the soft, inviting chairs.

"What a beautiful compact you have," one lady said to another. All eyes turned to look at the lady and her compact. It was very beautiful: made of gold with a small diamond on the lid, and her name engraved under the diamond.

Most of us hastily slipped our own modest compacts into our purses.

Some had imitation gold ones; and some, like myself, had brightly colored plastic ones.

The lady held up her expensive compact for all to see and said, "It was a gift from my husband on our first anniversary."

I think every woman there had some type of compact in her purse. The compact is something we think essential. We open it and find a mirror, a powder puff, some powder, and occasionally we slip a little change in our compact.

Every woman has a gift from God—the gift of life.

Like the compacts, our lives are not all alike. Some are born with silver spoons, some born to humble homes to know hardship and despair, most born just to conventional everyday homes.

All compacts have in common a mirror, a powder puff, and some powder.

All people have some things in common. We have the gift of life from God. We have the gift of influence. We have the gift of some talents. The way we respond to the gifts in our lives is the important factor.

Not a woman in that lounge walked over to the wastebasket and threw away her compact because it was not gold with a diamond on it. No, the cheapest one was still needed and useful to its owner.

We do not all have the same advantages. We do not all have the same talents. Yet we all have a purpose in life. Our duty is to find that purpose and live up to it.

IF YOU'VE GOT IT

If you've got it you don't have to flaunt it;
  It's really not needful to brag;
If advantage is yours, do not vaunt it;
  You don't have to wave victory's flag.

If you're free you don't have to proclaim it;
  The world is aware all the while;
If you're good, there's no need to declare it,
  Inferring you lead by a mile.

If you're rich, then you don't have to tell it;
  It's not a nice thing to rub in;
Never buy love of friends nor compel it
  But earn it if truly you'd win.

If you've power, then don't exercise it;
  A tyrant's despised by his slave;
If you've honor then don't compromise it;
  You're judged by the way you behave.

                    —J. T. Bolding

15

The Joy of Finding
the Stone Rolled Away

(Easter)

And they said among themselves, Who shall roll us away the stone from the door of the sepulchre? —Mark 16:3

There are many famous tombs over the world. The lavish wealth and artistic adornment of some cause world travelers to seek them out. A notable one is Tut-ankh-amen's in Egypt.

In Red Square at Moscow the remains of the famous leader Lenin are preserved by a mysterious process. People stand in long lines to pass by and see.

Yet in all of history there has never been a tomb so famous nor so talked about as the empty tomb of Christ.

Women going there with spices to preserve the body, thought of the obstacle in the way. Who will roll away the stone, for it is very great? What a surprise to find the stone rolled away and the body gone from the tomb!

On Easter Sunday we all stand in spirit before the tomb. Many of us still see great stones in front of the tomb—stones that prevent us from giving our whole service and life to the Lord who came forth victorious from that grave.

Who will roll away the stone? We must, by having faith in Christ, in His direction for our lives.

Picture the grief-stricken women, coming early in the day to perform a service of love. They were afraid and timid as they approached. They expected to find a great stone in front of the tomb, guarded by a Roman soldier. Yet their love was so great they determined to care for the body of Christ.

How surprised they were to find the stone rolled away. No soldier stood there to guard the door; so they went in.

Mark 16:6,7 tells us the story. There in the tomb they found a messenger, left by Christ to tell the news.

"He is risen!"

To know that Christ is risen means to have orders from Him. The young man sitting in the sepulchre gave them a command: "Go your way, tell his disciples."

They left and hurried away, much afraid. Aren't we so often afraid to go quickly and tell the story?

"He is risen" was the best news this world ever heard. Yet Mark 16:11 says that "they . . . believed not."

This news first discovered by women on Easter morning has transformed men. It has made heroes of cowards. It has given strength to the weak and power to the messengers.

Who will roll us away the stone? We will roll the stone away as we tell the joyful news. "He is risen."

When the disciples did believe, no words could express their joy. Death had been defeated, life and immortality had been brought to lighten a sinful world.

Brent, a teen-age boy, gave his parents much trouble. He would not stay in school and was often in trouble with the law. Finally he ran away from home. Because he was their son, the parents grieved and worried.

The parents belonged to a church but seldom bothered to go. On Easter Sunday they went, out of custom. The message touched their hearts and they were both truly converted.

After that Easter service their lives changed. They wanted so much a second chance for their son's love and respect. They realized all the fault had not been Brent's.

The parents counseled with their pastor. He offered a few suggestions about how to find the boy, but they were not really good ones.

The parents began to pray, asking God to lead them in the search for their son. God gave them a plan.

In a number of cities at the rescue missions the men in charge were surprised to get a letter asking them to read a message. The message was: "Brent, we have seen Jesus! Please come home. Life will be different."

Brent had spent his last cent. He was hungry and growing afraid. He had not known what the world was like away from his home town. He became so hungry he knocked on a door and asked for some food.

"Go down to the rescue mission. That is what it is for."

Tired, lonely, and afraid, Brent followed the woman's directions. He came to an old store building, converted into a meeting place for derelicts and drunks.

As the man in charge asked him to register his name, he noticed the name "Brent." That had been the name on the strange letter he had received earlier.

The men were required to listen to the service before they could eat. After the service the leader asked permission to read a message. "Brent, we have seen Jesus! Please come home. Life will be different." He noticed tears slipping under the lids of the teen-ager.

After the food had been served and the men assigned a cot for the night, the director called Brent into his office. "Brent, is this message from your parents?"

"It doesn't sound too much like them. They were not very religious." The boy hesitated.

"Would you like to go home and see?"

"Yes," Brent nodded. "I guess home was better than I thought."

The director began to talk to Brent. He explained to him the Easter story, and how the women and the disciples saw Jesus and how their lives were transformed. The boy in humble contrition trusted Christ. The man then called the phone number of the boy's parents.

When his father answered, Brent haltingly said: "Dad, I have seen Jesus too. I want to come home."

That is just one story of the countless millions whose lives were transformed after they saw Jesus.

After we have seen Jesus, we are given a command to "go quickly and tell others."

What do we have to tell? The best news in the world: Jesus is risen!

GOOD NEWS

Discouraged they were, so downcast and so blue;
The Saviour was dead, and now buried they knew;
Their hopes had been dashed so completely, 'twas true,
That even their memories brought little hope.

Discouraged and saddened by what had transpired;
Hard-stricken by grief, so exhausted and tired,
Disciples were scattered and fears were inspired:
They felt they had come to the end of their rope.

But then came the word: Christ has risen indeed;
To some, had appeared, and the word spread with speed;
The joyous disciples again took the lead
With visions that had an entirely new scope.

They walked, and their hearts overflowed with a song;
With high expectations they lived all day long,
For Christ was alive and the thought made them strong.
This joyous assurance had brought them new hope.

—J. T. Bolding

16

Peculiar Treasure

(Mother's Day)

For the Lord hath chosen Jacob unto himself, and Israel for his peculiar treasure. —Psalm 135:4

Can a woman forget her sucking child, that she should not have compassion on the son of her womb? —Isaiah 49:15

My son was going away to college. As I cleaned his room after his departure, I found so many peculiar treasures. There were those a boy gathers up along the way, feeling he is sure to need them for some important something in the future.

I put all the little polished rocks, a fancy ring, a bundle of assorted sizes of pencil lead into a box and placed it on the closet shelf.

Several years later, he wanted some peculiar thing and I told him to go and look in the box. How delighted he was with his old treasures. Each had a meaning from his past boyhood.

A mother is a peculiar treasure to any child. For to our mothers we owe our very existence.

What orphan child doesn't dream of finding a mother, doesn't dream of how wonderful it would be to have a mother.

God thought of the children of Israel as His peculiar treasure. In Exodus 19:5 they are called by that very name.

A child is a peculiar treasure to his parents, especially the mother. He may have a pug nose, straw-colored hair, freckles, even be mean; but his parents love him. He is different from all other children. He is theirs.

A child in school was asked by the teacher, "Bobby, why do you love your mother?"

The teacher expected the answer to be many things, such as, "She takes care of me, cooks for me," and so forth.

The little boy gave the truest answer of all. Looking at his teacher, he replied: "I love her because she is where I came from."

Wouldn't this world be great if every person could say, "I love God because He is where I came from!"

For any house to be a real home, there must be the wonder of a woman's love. God gave men strength to conquer the world. Men are the ones God assigns the task of taking care of the earth, but to mothers He assigned the task of love, encouragement, understanding.

Missionary friends of our family did not have children for a number of years. As they neared the age deadline for adopting children, there came an opportunity to pay an unfortunate girl's doctor bill and adopt her baby. Imagine their surprise when the baby turned out to be twins. The missionary couple were so happy and excited.

"Our whole life changed overnight. Those two helpless little babies took all our waking time and thoughts," the man told us.

"We would not give them back for anything in the world," the adoptive mother would declare.

Christianity has changed the status of mothers. Look at the condition of women before Christ came; then look at it now. Yet the Bible tells us about some wonderful mothers.

A few heroic mothers we might name from the Bible are Jochebed, mother of Moses; Eunice, the mother of Timothy; Hannah, the mother of Samuel; Mary, the mother of Jesus. On and on we could go. God recognized their worth, and the Holy Spirit impressed the writers to tell us about them.

We could look into the life of almost any great man in history and find he had a great mother.

Christianity has indeed made woman's lot easier; but women, on the other hand, have done a great deal for Christianity.

Our pastor was making a plea for people to help more with the finances of the church. A woman sitting near me said, "I will give a dollar more each week."

That might not sound like much to you as you read, but that dear woman lives on a very small pension. One more dollar a week meant she would have to do without something she needed, maybe even food.

Mothers have always been willing to sacrifice.

In Isaiah 66:13, God likens Himself to a mother: "As one whom his mother comforteth, ᴄo will I comfort you."

Our mothers are ⌐ peculiar treasure given to us by a loving heavenly Father. God suffered when His chosen people sinned. A mother suffers when her child goes astray or is disobedient.

Every person living has had a mother. Adam and Eve were the only people ever to live who did not have a mother. God created them, and because of that He loves the whole human race.

Mothers are only human and often make mistakes; yet we have definite obligations to our mothers. Exodus 20:12 says, "Honor thy father and thy mother: That thy days may be long upon the earth which the Lord thy God giveth thee." Paul called this the first commandment with promise.

Honor is a more comprehensive word than *obey*. We often obey a rule or order because we are afraid not to do so. We are to honor our parents. Honor represents respect, reverence, and love. We honor our parents when we make right choices and choose right companions. Proverbs 15:20 says, "A foolish man despiseth his mother."

Thomas Carlyle, in a letter to his mother, wrote: "If I had all the mothers I ever saw to choose from, I would have chosen you."

James A. Garfield said of his success in life: "If my mother could rise in the dead of night and pray for my recovery from sickness, my life must be worth something. Hearing her pray in an adjoining room, I then resolved to prove myself worthy of my mother's prayers."

So it is a peculiar treasure to have a mother. If she is a true Christian mother, then you are especially blessed.

It is a peculiar treasure to be the mother of a child. Not all women are so blessed.

All treasures require special handling. The owner of a large and precious stone will keep it in a bank vault. The owner of good property will take pains to see that the taxes are paid and the property papers in good shape.

The best way a mother can care for her peculiar treasure is by trusting that treasure, not to a bank vault, but to the care of God.

MOTHER APPRECIATION

Mother always has the time
To do the worthy deed,
To show the kindly interest
So many sadly need.

Mother always understands
And knows the better way,
Has the wisdom, patience, hope,
To bravely meet the day.

Mother gives, in measure full,
Her tender sympathy,
Sacred holds your confidence;
A faithful friend is she.

Mother finds unfailing strength
In Christ, her Saviour true,
This best Friend, in earth, or heaven,
With love commends to you.

—Unknown

17

The Thoughtful Are Thankful

(Thanksgiving)

Enter into his gates with thanksgiving, and into his courts with praise:
be thankful unto him, and bless his name. —Psalm 100:4

Thoughtful people are always thankful for the blessings they have. The blessing of life is one for which we can all be grateful.

A large family of children gathered around the dinner table. Spring had not yet arrived, and the food canned and stored for the winter had grown monotonous.

As they sat down, each began to complain. One was tired of turnips; another would like some fresh fried chicken in place of the cured ham.

The father, a hard-working man on the farm, listened in astonishment. "Children, children, what can you mean! Look at all the good food on the table, raised and preserved here on our own farm. Just last night I saw in the newspaper a picture of little children who were dying because they did not have even one bowl of the food you have so much of. I think we should all pray until we appreciate our blessings." The mother started a prayer. Then the father prayed. Then, one by one, they called on the children. As they prayed, the smell of the good food on the table grew almost unbearable, they were getting so hungry.

At last the smallest boy was called on. "Oh, Lord, forgive me. I love turnips and ham. If you will just let me eat before I starve to death smelling it, I'll never grumble again."

Soon the family started eating, laughing, and talking. During the years they spent on the farm growing up they never forgot to be thankful for God's blessings and the security of a home where food was plentiful.

Once I was in the hospital for two weeks. Of course, my every thought was: How soon will I get to go home?

At regular intervals the nurse came and took my temperature, blood pressure, and pulse rate.

"Why do you bother me so much with all of that?" I asked her.

"By your pulse, temperature, and blood pressure, the doctor judges how well you are progressing," she told me.

The Great Physician must often shake His head in sadness if He judges our spiritual condition by the thankfulness we show. Do our prayers often sound like a complaint department?

> *How can I ever fail to say*
> *A prayer of thanks each precious day.*
> *Since God has blessed me very much*
> *My love I'll show by deeds and such*
> *For Him along the way.*
>
> —J. T. Bolding

Ten-year-old Tom heard the teacher say, "What are you thankful for?" She asked each child to write a list. Tom thought about his grandfather and the stories he told of his early days. So his list read as follows:

I am thankful for the television; my own radio; a nice warm house, and no wood to cut; ice cream in the deep freeze; school and football; and for our new car.

The grandfather, nearly dozing in his comfortable chair when Tom read him his list, made a mental list of his own.

I am thankful for the trust of my grandchild; for the opportunities the world offers to him today; for the picture window to make my days indoors more interesting; and for the home God has for me when I leave this place.

As Tom read his list to his mother and father at the dinner table, the father thought of a list of his own. I am grateful for a job, and the opportunity to support my family. I am grateful for my wife and son and the joy we have together; and for the fact that I am able to take care of my father in his old age.

Tom's mother thought of all the security she felt in the love of her family and was grateful to God for them.

Thoughtful people are thankful, for our blessings come from a higher power in heaven and not from our own worthiness.

PROMPTERS TO GRATITUDE

If the raucous noise of commerce
  Makes no happy melody,
Then our need may be to converse
  With the desert's rhapsody.

If a rainbow we're beholding,
  There's a cloud nearby we know,
And without the showers enfolding,
  Lovely flowers cannot grow.

When a sign appears before us
  With instructions to detour,
We are prone to praise in chorus
  All good highways, that's for sure.

If the threat of sickness causes
  Gratitude for our good health,
Let us recognize these pauses
  As a part of our true wealth.

We so seldom count our blessings
  When there's no assenting woe,
And God's goodness start confessing
  Better when some fear we know.

                                        —J. T. Bolding

18

Gifts from Christ

(Christmas)

Who giveth food to all flesh: for his mercy endureth forever. —Psalm 136:25

THE CHRISTMAS SYMBOL

Only a manger, cold and bare,
Only a maiden mild,
Only some shepherds kneeling there,
Watching a little child;
And yet that maiden's arms enfold
The King of Heaven above;
And in the Christ-Child we behold
The Lord of Life and Love.

Only an altar high and fair,
Only a white-robed priest,
Only Christ's children kneeling there,
Keeping the Christmas feast;
And yet beneath the outward sign
The inward grace is given—

His Presence, who is Lord Divine
And King of earth and heaven.

—Unknown

Let us look at our Christmas gifts for a moment. We have spent more than we should; we have beautifully wrapped packages for loved ones and friends. Our houses are filled with sparkling decorations. Our town is all aglow with glitter and tinsel. People are going about in a big hurry, for there is so much to be done. Yet the day after Christmas it is all over, and gifts are either put away or put to use. Business must start up again as usual.

Christ has put some gifts under the great Christmas tree of life—gifts we often overlook.

The first gift I will mention is *rest*.

"Come unto me, all ye that labor and are heavy laden, and I will give you rest" (Matt. 11:28).

How tired we often feel after the rush of getting and giving things. We wonder if all the work was worth one day of celebration and festivities. Christ offers a gift of rest.

The second gift we find from our Lord is *the keys of the kingdom*.

"And I will give unto thee the keys of the kingdom of heaven: and whatsoever thou shalt bind on earth shall be bound in heaven: and whatsoever thou shalt loose on earth shall be loosed in heaven" (Matt. 16:19).

At Christmastime, teen-agers or young people ask for keys to new cars. Christ offers us the keys to a kingdom that will last forever.

Commentators say the authority to bind and to loose that Jesus gave His disciples was a power to fix with authority the moral standards and to determine the Christian creed. He promised that God Himself will ratify the "binding and loosing."

For just everyday people like myself, I think the keys of the kingdom are the following: the key of knowledge—knowledge of Christ, of salvation. Also the key of doctrine. We must tell people what the Bible teaches to the best of our ability. Then there is the key of discipline. We have the power to overcome evil, with God's help.

The third gift from Christ is the *power over evil spirits.*

"Behold, I give unto you power to tread on serpents and scorpions, and over all the power of the enemy: and nothing shall by any means hurt you" (Luke 10:19).

Christian people could turn the world upside down if they would only accept and use the gifts of Christ.

The fourth gift from Christ is *living water.*

"But whosoever drinketh of the water that I shall give him shall never thirst; but the water that I shall give him shall be in him a well of water springing up into everlasting life" (John 4:14).

A teen-aged girl, living in the hills of Kentucky, learned to know Christ one winter while she lived in the village and attended school. She tried to tell her parents about Christ, but they would not listen. During the summer back at her rural home she prayed often for them.

One of her tasks about the place was to walk to the spring and bring back buckets of water. Often she would stay in the quiet of the wood near the spring to pray for her unsaved parents and neighbors.

Several times her father noticed how long she stayed at the spring. One morning he followed at a distance, thinking to catch her with a neighborhood youth. He felt smug when he heard a voice. He stole closer and heard his child's voice.

"Oh, dear heavenly Father, please show me the way to win my father to Christ."

The father felt ashamed and crept quickly back to the house. When the girl came back he spoke to her. "You stayed so long. I hope you remembered to bring the water."

"Yes, father, I brought water from the spring; but I wish I could bring you the living water I know about."

The gift of living water is one you can constantly give away and still have plenty left.

The fifth gift Christ gave to us is *bread of heaven.*

"I am the living bread which came down from heaven: if any man eat of this bread, he shall live for ever: and the bread that I will give is my flesh, which I will give for the life of the world" (John 6:51).

The great preacher Charles H. Spurgeon once said: "But depend upon it, the only way to meet hunger is to get bread; and the only way to meet your soul's want is to get Christ, in whom there is enough and to spare, but nowhere else."

The sixth great gift Christ brought us is *eternal life*.

"And I give unto them eternal life; and they shall never perish, neither shall any man pluck them out of my hand" (John 10:28).

The seventh gift is the *legacy of peace*.

"Peace I leave with you, my peace I give unto you: not as the world giveth, give I unto you. Let not your heart be troubled, neither let it be afraid" (John 14:27).

What a wonderful gift! No worry that someone else might outshine us; just a joy and confidence that all is well.

"His clothes fell to the soldiers, his mother He left to John. But what should He leave His poor disciples that had left all for Him? Silver and gold He had none, but He left them that which was infinitely better—His peace" (Matthew Henry, Commentator).

At Christmas we give to others a gift approximately in value what we think they will give us. We give to those who we think will give to us.

I have listed seven great gifts from the greatest Giver of all. These are gifts that will make you happy, well fed, give life eternal, and fill your soul with a peace such as you have never known.

Yet there are countless numbers who refuse these gifts.

After a great storm had wrecked our city, an organization sent men around to see if they could help with the repair of damaged houses.

A representative came to the home of one of my friends. He told her that because she was a widow, had recently lost her job, and had no one to help her, his organization would pay up to $3500 for repairs on her house.

As she showed me through her newly refinished house, she said, "I almost didn't accept because I was afraid there was a catch to the offer."

How many people are afraid to accept the gifts of Christ because they fear there are "strings attached."

THE GIFT OF CHRISTMAS

The gift of Christmas—what
a wondrous thing!
This blessed day when joyous
carols ring
And peace on earth comes
nearer to each heart.
May Christmas radiance never
depart,
But shed its light throughout
the circling year
Within our homes, destroying
every fear.
Let us endeavor to be loving,
mild,
Remembering the gentle
Christmas Child.

—Unknown

19

I Remember Christmas

(A Christmas Poem)

I remember Christmas
Away back there when I was six.
Our socks were filled with fruit and
* nuts,*
And even candy sticks.
That year we got only one toy,
Or maybe there were two,
But we were just so very thrilled
We knew not what to do.

Our tree was just a cedar tree
We cut right on our farm.
And though it had no lights, you see,
It lent a certain charm.
With popcorn strung so gaily
By my sisters, mom and me.
And holly with red berries hung
Around for all to see.

Yes, I remember Christmas
The way it was away back then.

Why, the way we celebrate it now
Sometimes it seems a sin.
We listen to the merchant
Giving out his merry rill.
He thinks, "Oh, now's the time
That we must fill the till.
It's either now or never,
Get the business while you can."
Do you think he realizes
What big spending does to man?

Oh, the doctors get our money
After January first.
We pay for tranquilizers
That we carry in our purse,
To alleviate the mental stress
Brought on by Christmas spending.
Do you really think this type of life
Can have a happy ending?

Yes, I remember Christmas
Around the fire with dad and mother,
When the greatest gift that we all had
Was our love for one another.
And of Baby Jesus
As we read about his birth,
And how he grew to manhood
And walked about this earth.

As I remember Christmas
I hope that you do too.
And that you'll be very thoughtful
In all you say and do
To make this a holy Christmas
Full of Joy and Hope and Love,
As we celebrate the birthday
Of the Saviour up above.

—Mrs. Mont L. Jennings

20
Opportunity

(New Year's)

As we have therefore opportunity, let us do good unto all men, especially unto them who are of the household of faith. —Galatians 6:10

Isn't it strange that in the Bible we are often told to do good, but we are never told to seek power and fame. We often tell our young people they must go to certain schools because they are more powerful or more famous than others. We hold up before our children the fact that it is great to be powerful or famous. We forget to emphasize that it is noble just to help others and do good.

A small flag of the United States was owned by a little boy. On special days he carried it carefully to school and the teacher gave it a place of prominence on her desk.

The flag should have been happy with a teacher and twenty children to salute it. But through the window the little flag could see a large beautiful flag on a flagpole. The whole school marched out and stood at attention as they saluted the big flag.

"Oh, I wish I could be on the flagpole; then I could be honored by the whole school."

By some miracle the little flag was suddenly on top of the towering flagpole. But the flag was so small that no one passing below could see it at all. It was soon forgotten and lost. "What did I do wrong?" the little flag asked the one billowing just below.

"You thought of yourself and forgot the nation for which you stand."

Many Christians get drunk on power or greed for recognition, completely forgetting the Savior for whom they once said they stood.

In the New Testament we have a story of James and John desiring places of power in Christ's kingdom.

Christ wants His followers to be servants, not men of power or fame. Think of France: Napoleon was famous for his power, given him by his army of faithful men. Today Napoleon is not highly recognized.

Then there is another Frenchman, Pasteur. He served his country and the world by working long hours to learn how to fight disease germs. The good he accomplished lives on today and will go on being a blessing to mankind.

A New Year brings new opportunities. The question is: What kind of opportunities do we seek? Opportunities for helping others? Or opportunities for helping ourselves?

Each New Year means new problems in our world, in our churches, and in our communities. We each have a place to fill. The small flag had a place of service on the teacher's desk, but was not content to fill that place with dignity and honor.

Many a young minister has lost his power in the Spirit because he was not content to fill well the place God had given him. He constantly must be trying to seek a larger field.

Paul in our Scripture verse did not tell the Christians to seek opportunity for power or fame, but opportunity for doing good. If it is the will of our Lord, we will be elevated to places of greater service after we have proved ourselves in small places.

The New Year will bring you many opportunities—some for advancement in business or work, some for advancement in education. But most of all, you will have many, many opportunities for just plain old lending a helping hand to someone in need.

An old man seeking to ridicule a young pastor who called on him to tell him about Jesus said: "Are you the pastor of the First Baptist Church in Dallas?"

"No, sir, I am not, but I work for the same Boss, and He urged me to come and tell you about your need."

Every Christian person, regardless of church or position, works for the same Boss. Our Lord gave orders to the great and small before His ascension. You will find them in Matthew 28:19, 20. He offered the same reward and compensation to each person who follows His instructions.

I have often been amazed how many people come to church on the first Sunday in the year. When questioned, many will say: "I am determined to start the new year right."

OPPORTUNITY?

So many seek a glowing chance
To fill some famous place,
While, spotlight-centered they advance
In life's financial race:
They call it opportunity.

To be allowed to do one's best:
Achieve some useful thing;
To live each day with vim and zest,
And have the heart to sing:
Now that is opportunity!

To see a need, and help it some;
To know you've done the right;
To earn, assured you're not a bum,
And from life get delight:
That's worthwhile opportunity!

—J. T. Bolding

21

Ramblings on Love

(Valentine's Day)

Hatred stirreth up strifes: but love covereth all sins. —**Proverbs 10:12**

Though I speak with the tongues of men and of angels, and have not love, I am become as sounding brass, or a tinkling cymbal. —**I Corinthians 13:1**

Love covereth all sins! In other words, love is blind. Without love we are nothing!

One day a young mother was entertaining some friends. She had put her four-year-old in the backyard and told him to play until her company left.

After about an hour the little boy, very dirty from his play, came rushing into the house.

The company looked with raised eyebrows at the disheveled little boy.

"Mommie, I just got lonesome to see you." He ran to his mother and held up his arms for a hug.

After she had hugged him and kissed his face, he ran outside again.

"Isn't he just the sweetest one in all the world?" the young mother said.

"That ugly child sure proves love is blind," one lady stated to another as they went home together.

A young man in a small town was known for his careless way of driving. He always drove either a red or bright yellow car, and was recognized all over town. The guards at the school crossing always joked and would say: "Here comes Reckless Rayburn."

Then things changed. One September day Reckless Rayburn drove up to the school very slowly. He stopped near the door of the building, got out and helped a small, delicate child from the car. After kissing her good-bye he went back to the driver's side of the car.

"Are you sick, Mr. Rayburn?" one of the monitors from the previous year came to his side and asked. "You don't drive like yourself."

"You just saw the biggest piece of my heart walk up to that school," he told the questioner. "I must drive carefully with such a precious passenger."

We may be blind to the safety and needs of others and their children; but when a piece of our own heart is involved, our actions are different.

I once knew a large family of boys who grew up on a small farm in east Texas. All the boys left to work in the cities and make their way in the world. Until they were old men they would often make trips back to the little east Texas farm.

Why, I wondered, does it charm them so much? Their parents have been dead many years and the old farmhouse is vacant. The once fertile fields are now pasture land. When they lived there they had worked very hard to help make enough for the family to live on. Yet how they loved that old place.

Down the narrow little road leading off the highway, they would drive their fine cars. They would get out and walk about in the woods or draw water from the old well.

Then it came to me one day as I heard two of the brothers talking. Home, that home, represented love to them. There they had been born, there they had known the security of parents' love, security of being able to grow food and care for pets. The beautiful part of it all had stayed with them through the years. That home said to them: "There are arms around your shoulders."

Having been a minister's daughter and never having known the security of a permanent home, it took me a long time to understand. Yes, love is blind to the faults of a secure and happy home.

Love and the ability to love is God's greatest gift to mankind. The supreme way God showed His love for us is found in John 3:16. "For God so loved the world that he gave his only begotten Son, that whosoever believeth in him should not perish, but have everlasting life."

> *I've never been good,*
> *I've always been bad;*
> *So I wonder and I wonder*
> *At the blessings I've had!*

God's love does not wait for us to be worthy; it begins anew each morning with fresh blessings for us. It is hate that must have endings, never love.

Love is not a quality just for February 14, or June moons. Love is something we must carry in our hearts always. Love is expressed in many different ways. Love is spontaneous.

One Sunday afternoon a young mother was walking near a new housing project with her two small daughters. In the manner children have of running ahead, the little girls ran to a gravel pit.

The mother heard a strange sound; and running forward, saw gravel engulf her children. She began to dig away the gravel with her bare hands. Soon her hands were bleeding and torn, but she went right on tearing the gravel away from her babies. At last when they were free enough to breathe, she fainted from fright.

Part of the flesh never grew back on the mother's hands, and they were very ugly and deformed as they healed. As they grew old enough to understand, the girls would say, "Mommie, you have beautiful hands; they saved our lives."

Love often gives us superhuman strength in a crisis. Love may be blind to faults, but true love is ever eager to serve and show one's affection.

If we truly love someone, we want to give to him, to serve him, rather than have him serve us. That type of love is what makes a happy home—a husband and wife each wanting to do things for the other.

God wanted to give us a supreme gift in His Son, yet I Corinthians 2:8 tells us there are greater things yet to come. "But as it is written, Eye hath not seen, nor ear heard, neither have entered into the heart of man, the things which God hath prepared for them that love him."

We must write on the hearts of those we meet each day a poem of love, a living testament that our hearts are filled with love and not hate.

In youth we think romantic love is the greatest kind of love in the world. In times of crises we feel the person who loves enough to act in an unselfish manner is the great symbol of love. Yet the world is filled with people who never perform great or daring feats for a loved one, but just live day after day in a quiet way, showing love by kindness and service.

Often we are making deposits in the bank of love and do not realize it. A friend of mine called me to wish me a happy birthday.

"I am very busy today," she said. "I am cooking lunch for an old friend of my mother's. Mother used to visit her when I was a child, and she was always so kind to me. Now she is old and helpless, and I want to be good to her."

Fear of not being loved makes life unbearable for older people. They do not wish for fine gifts from their children; they want the finest gift of all—love.

The following story is just a fairy tale, but it explains something about love.

Queen Willa lived in a castle tower. She was not allowed to go outside the castle walls except on occasions of pomp and parades. Then she must stay in a carriage and never be touched by the common people of her kingdom.

One day as she looked out of the tower window, she saw children playing in the street outside the castle wall. They were singing a song about love.

She called her lady-in-waiting to the window. "What do they mean about this word *love?*" she asked.

The poor lady-in-waiting tried to explain what love meant. She had known nothing but orders and harsh words, so she could not explain love to the queen.

Then the queen called her chamberlain. "Tell me what they mean by 'we've got love.' "

The chamberlain thought and thought. He did not know about love, for he was very greedy. He often stole things from the queen.

"Prepare me for an appearance. I will go outside and ask the children. They have something I know nothing about; and since I am queen, I want some of everything."

Outside the palace walls the queen's herald ordered all the children to come near, but not near enough to touch.

"Bring me some of your love," she ordered.

"We do not know how. It is just a song we were taught by Roddie the crippled orphan."

"Where is Roddie? I must know what love is!" the queen demanded.

"Roddie is at Mrs. Longfelter's house now. He takes care of her babies at this time of day so she can go to work," the children told her.

At last the queen sent her lady-in-waiting to stay with the children while Roddie came to talk to her.

"Now, little boy, tell me what love is. I want to own some," the queen ordered.

"Oh, but my dear Majesty," the little boy's voice quivered, "there is a secret to getting love. You cannot buy it at a store or even take it by force."

"But all the children say you have more love than any child in town. How is that possible, seeing you are an orphan child and are wearing rags?"

"I do not know why all the people are so kind to me." The little boy pulled his ragged coat close about him.

"What do you do all day? I will find the secret." The queen stamped her foot.

Roddie began his story. "Before daybreak each morning I get up from my cot in the widow Major's kitchen. I build a fire and put on water to heat for her morning tea. If she has enough, she gives me a little sip and a small piece of bread. But she is very poor." He was growing tired. "Then I run over to the cobbler's shop. There I sit by his fire and read to him from a book, for he never went to school. He works at finishing some shoes. Often he gives me a whole cup of tea and a small piece of meat. Then I hurry to the school building. There I help the teacher bring in the wood for the day and dust the benches. She helps me with my lessons before the others come. At noon time I help Jason with his lessons, for he needs special help. His father is rich and he has a big lunch; so he gives me something to eat. After school I must go to Mrs. Longfelter's and care for the children."

"Aren't you jealous when you see all the children run and play and you must work?" the queen asked.

"Oh, no, I am happy. You see, they are my friends and I am glad when they have fun."

"I could have you put in prison because you will not tell me what love is." The queen was very cross. "I want love."

"I will show you what love is." The ragged child went closer to the queen and touched her hand. "My mother told me the secret as she died."

"Tell me quickly and you will not go to prison."

"If you want to be loved, you must love others." The child looked at his queen with a bright smile. "I will love you, dear queen."

"How can I love others?"

"Think of all the good things you can do for them and start out to do them," he told her.

"Oh, I will, I will. Go, chamberlain, and buy this boy a warm suit and coat." She began to smile. "Come back tomorrow, all of you; and I will think of something good to do for everyone."

That lesson on love is the reason Queen Willa rules over the happiest kingdom in the world. The little crippled orphan taught her the secret of love.

Did you learn the secret?

22

Let's Think About Love

Beloved, let us love one another: for love is of God; and every one that loveth is born of God, and knoweth God. —I John 4:7

In the month of February we always think of love for people. For some reason we think of Valentine's Day as a time to show our love in a special way. But Christians should always be thinking of love for others. In the Scripture verse above, we are told that love is of God.

The first love we know in this life is the love our mother shows us when we are babes in arms. How a little one will cry to get the attention of a loving mother or father. To cry is the only way they know to make themselves heard. How they cuddle up and become quiet at the soothing of the mother!

For many of us, our second great love comes when we give our hearts to Jesus and dedicate our lives in His service. "Seeing ye have purified your souls in obeying the truth through the Spirit unto unfeigned love of the brethren, see that ye love one another with a pure heart fervently" (I Peter 1:22).

A young woman was engaged to a young man at the beginning of World War II. The boy's parents objected very much to the engagement. He was their only son, and they wanted him always to stay home and take care of them. The girl was sad and discouraged. Yet she knew she loved the young man dearly.

The draft board called the man into service. The sweethearts decided to be married before he left for camp. The parents objected so strongly that the couple did not go on with their wedding plans.

In just a short time the man was sent overseas. The parents were distraught. They had to learn to do many things for themselves.

The girl was heartbroken. She felt the parents had been unfair and unjust. But she was different from the parents in one way: she was a devout Christian. Each day she read her Bible and prayed. One day a Scripture verse seemed to speak just to her: "See that ye love one another with a pure heart fervently."

"I have failed to love Bill's parents with a pure heart," she said. "I will ask God to forgive me."

So she took her latest letter from Bill and went to his parents' home.

At first they were very cold and almost rude to her, but gradually they began to treat her better. She won them with love and kindness.

This story does not have a happy ending. Bill was killed in the Battle of the Bulge. The young woman married someone else and moved to another state. Many times the parents thought how nice it would have been if Bill had been married and had left them a grandchild.

The third great love we must know and show is our love for others. God loved us enough to send His only Son. We must love those about us. Christ died for all—the good and the bad. We must seek to love and win all.

My husband has a blind aunt. For many years when anyone came into the home with something new she would say, "Let me feel of it." The different members of the family would try to describe things to her, but she always wanted to feel.

We can describe Christ's love to others, but they cannot really know it until they have felt it in their own hearts.

The great preacher Dwight L. Moody used to tell the story about his first trip away from home.

He was only about ten years old when his older brother took him into town to work. The first day was so sad and lonely for him. Then an old man came along. He saw the little boy with traces of tears on his cheeks. He stopped and talked to him. He told Dwight how God had sent His only Son away from His beautiful home in heaven to come to earth and help others. When he had finished talking, he gave the homesick boy a new copper penny.

As the old man talked, he held his large hand on the head of the child. A gentle touch of love and concern. Moody said for many years he remembered the kind touch of that hand on his head.

So we might gather that the fourth great kind of love is the love of doing for others. The old man gave away a penny and a touch on the head, and it lasted for many years.

We have no way of knowing how long a kind word will last. We have no way of knowing what tragedy or disaster a kind touch or act may prevent in one who is downcast and blue.

At different periods of life we have need of different kinds of love. A baby needs its mother; a young man or woman needs the love of a sweetheart; parents growing old need the love and care of their children; all people need the respect and love of their neighbors.

All these kinds of love are great and important; yet the love of Christ is greater and more precious than any other. The love of Christ is always ours to depend on. We need never have fear of loss or disagreement. Christ is ours always and forever when we give our hearts to Him.

All people think about love. Some think of how to get it; some think of how to give it. Many never discover that in order to get, one must give. Christ gave His life for us. Are we giving Him the love He deserves?